BOUNCE BACK

TO

SUCCESS

HOW TO OVERCOME AND STEER THROUGH ADVERSITY

BRIAN TRACY
AND
OTHER LEADING ENTREPRENEURS
AND PROFESSIONALS

Foreword by:
Shahab Anari,
International High Performance Expert

NORTHSTAR SUCCESS

BOUNCE BACK TO SUCCESS: HOW TO OVERCOME AND STEER THROUGH ADVERSITY

For bulk orders for promotions, fundraising and educational use, please contact North Star Success for special discounts. Book excerpts can be created as needed.

Published by North Star Success Inc.

🌐 www.northstarsuccess.com
✉ support@northstarsuccess.com
📞 +1 647 479 0790

FOREWORD

When faced with difficult times, we have only two choices:

- Wait for the world to go back to normal and let outside circumstances dictate our destiny.

- Or gain the strategies needed to create our own success.

Challenges and adversities are a given in life. It's not a matter of 'if' they happen; rather, it's a matter of 'when'. We will all encounter crises and setbacks in our lives. The key question is, "How are we going to respond to those roadblocks along the way?" Brian Tracy and his co-authors in this book have shared their insights about how we can steer through and overcome when adversity strikes.

Every author in this book has underscored the importance of resilience as the core skill that can help us navigate through life's challenges. And I have personally come to understand this concept in my own life, too. Let me tell you a brief story:

I was sitting alone in my doctor's cold office watching her read my test results. I already knew that something was wrong. I'd had inflammatory bowel disease for three years and this felt like a flare up. It turns out it was worse than normal.

"I'm quite concerned about you, Shahab," she said. "This might develop into cancer."

My heart dropped, and my head went dizzy. When I heard the word cancer, my first thought was my wife and child. My second thought was about the things I might never do.

I had dance classes I wanted to take....

Okay, thoughts in times of stress can be a little strange.

My doctor told me I was actually doing too much - particularly when it came to work. I was pushing myself beyond the bounds of good health.

One year before, my wife and I had immigrated to Canada in the hope of creating a better future. Back home, I was a noted language instructor, but in Canada I was planning for a change. Immigration was the perfect opportunity for me to shift gears and follow my new passion - coaching people to become more successful in their lives.

I wanted to succeed as quickly as I could so I poured a lot of time, energy, and money into building a successful coaching practice. For me that meant 12-hour workdays – seven days a week. You can imagine how much fun I was back then!

All the tension and pressure began to take its toll. I started to get anxiety attacks, and I almost fell into depression.

I needed to become truthful with myself and find out why things weren't working out. When I slowed down to take an honest look at my situation, I realized something extremely important. The idea of being a generalist coach who posted motivational stuff on social media had sounded like a good strategy at first, but it was not yielding significant results. I needed to discover my own genius. A genius that could help solve a specific problem for a specific type of person.

To discover my genius, I needed to do a lot of soul searching, spend a lot of time getting feedback from people who knew me, and read a lot of books. This required that I have the ability to be patient and continue in the face of the tough times I was going through. In other words, it required RESILIENCE.

So, I tapped into my resilience reserves that I knew had helped me in the past:

Although I failed to pass the 'gifted children's test' as a young kid, I gradually made my way up the academic ladder and came first among more than one million contenders in the fierce nation-wide University Entrance Exam in my country of birth in 1997.

I trained as a medical doctor, but I was not passionate about medicine as a career. Therefore, after graduation, I made the long difficult transition to become a speaker/trainer, which took me more than 10 years to accomplish. Thankfully, I have now served people in 19 different countries.

I knew what I needed to do. I humbled myself, became a student of business, spent a lot of time, money, and energy on building my personal brand, and over time, the world responded. Not only did my business grow like crazy over the next few years, but my health improved. I also started helping a lot of other ambitious individuals along the way. To say this process changed my life for the better is an understatement.

This book is all about the superpower of RESILIENCE. It's about the ability to bounce, rather than break, in the face of adversity. In this book, Brian Tracy and other leading entrepreneurs and professionals from around the world have shared their inspiring stories and golden insights on how anyone can overcome adversity and bounce back to success.

I hope you enjoy reading this book, and maybe some day, my company will share YOUR story and insights in a book like this!

Shahab Anari, MD
🌐 www.shahab.website
🌐 www.northstarsuccess.com
Publisher of Bounce Back to Success
International Speaker and Author

Contents:

Your Most

Valuable Asset

Brian Tracy

Your Most Valuable Asset

Brian Tracy

You have the ability, right now, and for the rest of your career, to make all the money you want, no matter what is happening in the world around you. You simply need to learn the so-called "secrets of success," and apply them regularly and consistently.

Life is a series of ups and down, like the weather, never going on the same way indefinitely. Your ability to manage the inevitable challenges and crises of life is the key to personal leadership, and to bouncing back from whatever problems and difficulties life hands you.

Your Most Valuable Asset

What you are about to learn changed my life and it will change yours as well, in a positive way. This single concept took me from struggle and worry about money to financial success and independence, and it will do the same for you, as well, and far faster.

When I first heard the question, "What is your most valuable asset?" I immediately thought of my car, my furniture, my house, my investments and money in the bank. And I didn't have much of any of them.

But these are not your most valuable financial assets. Your most valuable asset is your "earning ability." It is your ability to earn money each day, week, month and year. It is your ability to enter into a competitive market place and use your acquired and accumulated talent, skills, intelligence and ability to achieve results for which people will pay you good money.

It is also your ability to deal successfully with the unexpected setbacks and reversals of daily life.

Bounce Back from Failure

You could lose your house, your car, your job, and all your money, ending up penniless on the street. But as long as you have maintained your earning ability and were able to enter back into the marketplace, you could pump tens of thousands of dollars into your life. You could make it all back, and more besides.

Because of our rapid changing economy, and the continuing obsolescence of your knowledge and skills, your earning ability can be either an "appreciating asset" or a "depreciating asset".

If your earning ability is an "appreciating asset," this means that you are becoming increasingly valuable every week, month and year. You are continually upgrading your existing skills, and adding new knowledge and skills that enable you to get even better results for which people will pay you even more money.

For most people, who are not aware of the importance of their earning ability, their existing skills are a "depreciating asset." It is continually losing value, year by year, because the individual is not getting better and better at what he does. Even worse, most people are getting worse in the essential skills required by their jobs. They are progressively worth less and less.

Pat Riley, the basketball coach, said, "If you're not getting better, you're getting worse." No one stays in the same place in a time of rapid change or economic setbacks.

Peter Drucker said, "The only skill that will be of lasting value in the 21st century will be the skill of learning new skills. All other skills will become obsolete with the passing of time."

Your Most Precious Resource

Here is another question: What is your most precious resource?

It is not something tangible or material, like your bank account, investments or your home. Your most precious resource is actually your "time."

Your time represents your life itself. Your life is made up of the minutes and hours of each day. Once time has passed, it can never be retrieved. Once a minute or an hour has gone by, that amount of your life has passed as well.

Your Best Investment

One more question: What is your very best investment?

Answer: The very best investment you can make is to invest your time into increasing your earning ability. There is nothing that will improve the quality of your life, boost your income, and enable you to enjoy a better lifestyle than by "getting better" at what you do today to earn your income.

You have heard about the 80/20 Rule. This rule, the "Pareto Principle," says that 20% of your activities will account for 80%

of your results, 20% of the things that you do in your work will account for 80% of your income.

This rule also says that the top 20% of people in any society earn and control 80% of the wealth. The bottom 80% of money earners have to struggle and get by on whatever is left over by those in the top 20%.

Why does this happen? Why do some people earn several times the income of others? As it happens, everyone starts off roughly the same. We have roughly the same education, intelligence and opportunity. Like a marathon, we all line up at the starting line and then the gun goes off. In the months and years ahead, some people move to the front, the bulk stay in the middle, and many people fall to the back, not even completing the race until everyone has gone home.

Income Gap versus Skills Gap

There is a good deal of talk today about the "income gap" in our society. But Gary Becker, the 1993 Nobel Prize winning economist, has pointed out that we do not have an "income gap" as much as we have a "skills gap."

The people in the top 20% are simply those who have learned the essential skills that they need to achieve a high level of earning ability. The people in the bottom 80% are those who, having had the same opportunity, failed to develop those skills.

Many people have gone from rags to riches by realizing this critical fact, and then dedicating themselves to become very good in what they do. You must do the same.

Every person who is serious about their future, especially their financial future, should commit to being in the top 10% of their field. What we have found is that, anything less than a commitment to excellence condemns a person to being mediocre.

Your Default Setting

It seems as if there is a "default setting" on human performance. If you don't decide to become the best, you simply become average. Nobody sets off in life to be "average" or below. But by failing to dedicate yourself totally, especially in the formative years of your career, to becoming absolutely excellent at what you do, you automatically default into the bottom 80%, where you worry about money all your life.

In the 21st century, you are a "knowledge worker." You do not work with your physical body, making and moving things. You work with your mind, applying your intelligence and personality to your world to make a valuable contribution that others will pay you for. The key to becoming an effective knowledge worker is for you to continually upgrade your knowledge and skills in the work that you have chosen to do.

Key Result Areas

In each job, there seems to be about five to seven key result areas that account for performance, effectiveness and results in that job. You may perform dozens of small tasks in the course of a day or a week, but there are seldom more than five to seven key tasks that determine your success or failure.

For example, in management, the seven key result areas are: 1) Planning; 2) Organizing; 3) Staffing; 4) Delegating; 5) Supervising; 6) Measuring; 7) Reporting. Your success as a manager can largely be determined by how well you do your job and perform these functions in each area.

In selling, for example, the Seven Key Result Areas are: 1) Prospecting and getting appointments; 2) Establishing rapport and trust; 3) Identifying customer needs accurately; 4) Presenting your products persuasively; 5) Answering customer objections and concerns; 6) Closing the sale and getting the customer to take action; 7) Getting resales and referrals from satisfied customers.

This is what we have discovered: Your weakest key skill in your field determines the height of your income and your success. Your weakest essential skill is what holds you back from performing at your very best in all of the other areas. By identifying your weakest skill, and then becoming excellent in that area, you can often surge ahead rapidly in your career and move up into the top 10%.

Your Most Important Skill

How do you determine the skill that can help you the most? You ask this question: "What one skill, if I was absolutely excellent at, would help me the most to double my income?"

If you are not sure about your answer to this question, you must find out as quickly as possible. Ask your boss. Ask your coworkers. Ask your friends. Ask your customers. But you must know the answer to this question or you cannot move ahead in your career. It is impossible for you to get into the top 10% in your field unless you know with great clarity which skill, or lack of skill, is holding you back.

Once you have determined the one skill that can help you the most, write it down as a goal using these words: "I am absolutely excellent at this particular skill by (such and such a date)."

Then, make a list of everything you could do to develop this skill. Organize the list by sequence and priority. What do you need to do before you do something else? What is more important and what is less important? A list of activities, organized by sequence and priorities, becomes a plan. With a goal and a plan, you will start to make more progress in your life than you can imagine today.

The next step is for you to take action immediately on your new goal, that of becoming excellent in an area where you are still weak. Then, to complete your success, you must do something every single day that makes you a little bit better.

Read a little bit in your field. Listen to audio programs in your car. Attend seminars and courses. And most of all, practice, practice, practice until you finally reach the top.

Join the Top 10%

When I first learned that I would have to be in the top 10% in my field in order to enjoy the highest possible income, I immediately felt discouraged and disappointed. I had never been good at anything before. I had been kicked out of high school in the 12th grade and had worked at laboring jobs for several years. When I got into sales, I knocked on hundreds of doors, cold-calling, and made almost no sales at all.

Then, a top sales professional told me that I would have to be in the top 20% of our field to really achieve all the riches and rewards of the selling profession. It was after that that I learned something that changed my life. I learned that everyone who is in the top 20% started in the bottom 20%. Everyone who is doing well was once doing poorly. Everyone who is at the top of their field today was at one time not even in their field, and did not even know that their field existed.

Here is a great discovery. All business skills are learnable. All sales skills are learnable. All management skills are learnable. All business building and entrepreneurial skills are learnable. All success skills and money-making skills are learnable.

Everyone who is good at them today was at one time poor in every area. But they made a decision, set a goal, made a plan, and worked on it, over and over again, until they mastered the skill. And what hundreds of thousands and millions of other people have done, you can do as well.

No One Smarter Than You

Remember, no one is smarter than you and no one is better than you. If someone is doing better than you today, it simply means that they have learned the essential skills they need before you have. And anything anyone else has done, you can do as well.

When you follow this formula, concentrating on your most important skills, and disciplining yourself to persist until you have mastered that skill, you will open up your whole life. You will put your career onto the fast track. You will increase you earning ability rapidly.

As you get better and better at a key skill, your self-esteem will increase. Your self-image will improve. You will like and respect yourself more, and you will be liked and respected more by the people around you. You will feel a tremendous sense of personal power and pride as you get better and better at what you do.

Sooner or later, in a month, six months, or a year, you will have mastered that key skill. Then what do you do? You repeat the process!

Once again, you ask, "Now, what one skill will help me the most to double my income?"

You write it down, make a plan, and work on it every day. You turn yourself into a lifelong do-it-to-yourself project.

Fast Track to Success

Thousands of chief executive officers of large and small companies have been asked, "What qualities would most mark a person for rapid promotion in your company?"

Fully 85% of them give the same answer. They say: "The most valuable people in my company are those who set priorities, work on their most important tasks, and get their most important job done quickly and well."

As you develop new skills, increasing your earning ability, your levels of knowledge and skill, you must then apply what you know to getting more important jobs done quickly.

There is nothing that will cause you to stand out in your field more than by developing a reputation as a hard worker who does things quickly and well.

In a short period of time you will become the "go-to person" in your company. When your boss, or other key people, want or need something done quickly, they will come to you. Along with these additional responsibilities will come additional authority, opportunity and increased income.

Your goal should be to become one of the most effective, most competent, most respected and highest paid people in your business.

The good news is that there are no limits to what you can accomplish, and how far you can go, when you dedicate your working life to continually increasing your earning ability. You will soon become one of the highest paid people in your field.

Your Most
Valuable Asset

Author's Bio

Brian Tracy is Chairman and CEO of Brian Tracy International, a company specializing in the training and development of individuals and organizations. He is among the top speakers, trainers, and seminar leaders in the world today.

Brian Tracy has consulted for more than 1,000 companies and addressed more than 5,000,000 people in 5,000 talks and seminars throughout the U.S., Canada and 82 other countries worldwide. As a keynote speaker and seminar leader, he addresses more than 250,000 people each year.

He has studied, researched, written, and spoken for 35 years in the fields of economics, history, business, philosophy and psychology. He is the top selling author of 80 books that have been translated into 42 languages.

Brian has written and produced more than 1000 audio and video learning programs, including the worldwide, best-selling Psychology of Achievement, which has been translated into 28 languages.

He speaks to corporate and public audiences on the subjects of Personal and Professional Development, including the executives and staff of many of America's largest corporations. His exciting talks and seminars on Leadership, Sales, Self-Esteem, Goals, Strategy, Creativity and Success Psychology bring about immediate changes and long-term results. His "2-Day MBA" transforms business owners and companies.

Prior to founding his company, Brian Tracy International, Brian was the Chief Operating Officer of a $265 million dollar development company. He has had successful careers in sales and marketing, investments, real estate development and syndication, importation, distribution, and management consulting. He has conducted high level consulting assignments with several billion-dollar corporations in strategic planning and organizational development.

He has traveled and worked in 120 countries on six continents and speaks four languages. Brian is happily married and has four children. He is active in community and national affairs and is the President of three companies headquartered in San Diego, California.

Brian is the president of Brian Tracy International, an internet-based company that helps businesses of all sizes increase their sales and profitability by implementing the best practices of top businesses worldwide.

To learn more about Brian Tracy, please visit his website at ⊕ www.briantracy.com

Be Fearless

When Making Decisions

Mehdi Aghaloo

Be Fearless When Making Decisions
Mehdi Aghaloo

Changing careers may never come with ease and peace, and the moment I decided to do that, I was overwhelmed. After passing many a long, sleepless night, I awoke one morning and made up my mind to finally take that huge step. I had given it enough consideration. Though it was scary, I felt compelled to make this decision, instead of losing my passion to time and tide.

Getting Off to a Good Start

I set foot in Canada in 2013 to continue doing what I was good at back in Iran. I have a master's degree in Structural Design, and I worked in the construction business in Iran. Upon my arrival in Canada, I quickly started to obtain the required licenses and work permits, resulting in the establishment of a design and construction engineering company in 2015.

My company's services covered a wide variety of activities, mainly focusing on two lines of business. The first was designing residential, commercial and industrial buildings, where we helped our clients to modify existing buildings or tear them down and rebuild them from scratch. Our primary job was designing the structure, preparing the final blueprints, and securing the ultimate building permit package to be provided to the executive team. Secondly, we handled investors who wanted to enter the construction business. As they had absolutely no idea how to build a building, we helped them navigate their projects from square one to their ultimate completion.

From 2015 to 2019, I managed to create a strong network, a thriving business, and a trusting customer base. Specifically, from 2017 to 2019 we experienced sharp growth, and the market was irresistibly good for doing a variety of jobs in the field of construction.

During this period, I began to notice a gap which time and again made us lose potential customers and projects. More often than not, the problem was that investors found themselves with a lack of financial resources to fund new projects. This would make them shy away from the whole process and invest in another business. This was a problematic issue, negatively affecting them and us, because both parties were losing precious opportunities.

I realized we needed to add a new dimension to our business and make it the one-stop solution for anyone who wanted to do construction, with services ranging from simple investment to complete involvement in the design and construction process. We needed to add mortgage services, so our clients would be able to bridge any gaps between their current financial status and their desired ability to start a project.

As I started to dig into how the mortgage industry works, I became highly interested in it, so much so that if had a time machine, I would go back and choose finance as my major. Before this, I never thought financing projects would become so attractive to me in and of itself. I had been active in my professional field for fifteen years, and over time, I came to realize this was not what I wanted to keep doing in my retirement years. On the other hand,

I kept finding myself trying to present financial strategies and solutions to the clients who needed them for their projects. I would research and come up with those solutions, happy that I could help the clients with their complicated problems.

I also had the desire to develop my own status into a more financially successful one, particularly to enable my family to have an even more comfortable life in the future. As I was already well-established in the construction business, it felt like an ideal time to add a new dimension to my professional life. Many exciting ideas filled my mind, and I definitely wanted to enter the finance field, particularly the mortgage industry. I considered leaving my current business altogether. That was a terrifying thought, because I didn't have the required expertise yet, and I also had an uncertain future ahead.

Reservations in the Dead of Night

Numerous reservations kept me awake at night. Is a change really necessary? Am I able to create a strong network again? What if I am not able to make enough money for my family? Many such concerns rained down upon me night and day. I was obsessively considering all aspects and consequences of my new idea. I already had a great business, satisfactory income and a strong network. I was just growing bored and unhappy with the mundane routines of a job which apparently didn't challenge me that much anymore.

This was exactly the cause of my initial inertia in making that huge decision. My current work role had created a comfort zone beyond which I was highly reluctant to even look, let alone leap into and thrive. Whenever I thought of changing my status quo,

I became scared. What I needed was to become fearless when making decisions, which comes far easier in words than in action.

What does it mean to be fearless when making decisions? I have found the answer to this question. First, you need to open your eyes to the details of the path you are preparing to take. A representative example is analyzing different aspects of a business before starting it, ranging from set-up costs to its income potential, from strategies to tactics and daily plans. I have come to realize the key to acting fearlessly is to carefully and clearly outline and analyze, before deeply considering all implications and dimensions of a decision.

There are two significant points to keep in mind. First, you should try to minimize the probability of being surprised by events that you have neglected to consider when making plans. If you make a strenuous effort to see what the future clearly looks like after your decision, what paths open up in front of you and what obstacles appear, you will be courageous when making decisions. Second, never forget that, no matter what market you enter, it is going to be a competitive one, and no one is going to make it any easier for you. Sometimes, failures happen due to the competition playing the game better, but you can always learn and improve with each new venture. In any case, you need to have a comprehensive development plan, inclusive of short-, mid-, and long-term goals and the detailed routes leading to them.

An Inquiry into the Unknown

This strategy is exactly how I started. I listed a number of questions I had in mind and began what later became a complex and exciting inquiry into the nature and dynamics of the mortgage market. The first questions were quite simple, ranging from "How does the mortgage industry work?" to "What market share can I initially secure without any network?" I considered everything, the required permits and licenses, ways to provide my customers with a variety of services, routes of developing the new business from my existing network, and many more angles. I needed to make my own detailed and clear plan, which would lead to meeting all kinds of customer needs. At that time, I was only aware of one type of mortgage; now I was going to learn about all the other types and decide which ones I could provide to my customers.

One way to find answers to my questions was benefiting from the advice of established professionals in the field. I located these experts and had numerous conversations regarding my questions, which enlightened me on a variety of levels and gave me a clear vision of the journey on which I was about to embark. I was an active listener during all the conversations, passionately and intently gleaning invaluable information which they generously provided. One of the precious lessons I learned throughout my interviews with successful professionals in the field was that being an active listener makes people more enthusiastic to impart their wisdom to you.

Having gathered lots of information, I was now going to enter the second stage of my research, categorizing the information with regards to the different phases of business development. When organized into categories and built into larger blocks of knowledge, the information would definitely minimize the probability of me making mistakes and errors in the future.

I realized, throughout my research, I was dealing with two facets of risk. The first was inside the circle of things I could control. The second was out of my control. For instance, communication with customers, marketing, and establishing a sales strategy I could control. But the possibility of the licensing process taking more time than expected was in the realm of external organizations, and issues like that I could do nothing about.

At this point, I did a SWOT (Strengths, Weaknesses, Opportunities and Threats) analysis to further understand my position in the market, things I could do, things I should do, and things posing a risk to me. I needed to clearly understand what opportunities lay ahead and how I could take advantage of them without risking too much. At this stage, I decided to leave a sum of money in reserve, because I knew getting the business off the ground would require a considerable amount of money, and I did not want that to be an issue. Instead, I'd rather focus on work issues, such as developing strategies and attracting new clients.

One of the best decisions I made at this stage was to benefit from the guidance of a professional coach, in whom I put my faith and trust. The coach's knowledge of the complexities awaiting me on my path was absolutely stunning, and our sessions helped me immensely, shedding light on dark spots previously unknown to me. Through using professional coaching, my analytic style became more sophisticated, and my knowledge of the market grew clearer. I eventually managed to draw up a detailed business plan, a precise blueprint with the potential of allaying any fear that arose.

Throughout this journey, which is still ongoing, I learned an invaluable lesson. Fear and reservations can decrease the quality of our decisions to unbelievably low levels. Fears find you time and again, and no good comes from them.

On the other hand, being fearless when making decisions provides you with high-quality, motivated, rich decisions that are based in sheer passion. Fearlessness comes from your efforts to deliberately drive fear out of your conscious and unconscious minds, by increasing your clarity of vision regarding the future. These decisions, coupled with your true capabilities, can deeply change your life for the best.

Be Fearless When Making Decisions

Author's Bio

Mehdi Aghaloo, M.Sc., P.Eng. can find you
money for your real estate needs! He is a mortgage professional
who serves his clients in the Greater Toronto Area. Whether you're
looking for a residential/commercial mortgage, a business loan, or
a construction loan, Mehdi can help you with his vast knowledge
of the financial world and his large network of lenders.

One of Mehdi's strengths is his unique ability to secure construction loans for builders and investors. After long years of successful
experience as a structural engineer, he noticed a gap which time
and again made him lose potential customers and projects. More
often than not, the problem was that investors found themselves
with a lack of financial resources to fund new projects. This would

make them shy away from the whole process.

He, therefore, realized he needed to add a new dimension to his business and make it a one-stop solution for anyone who wanted to do construction, with services ranging from simple investment to complete involvement in the design and construction process. He decided to add mortgage services, so his clients would be able to bridge any gaps between their current financial status and their desired ability to start a project.

If you're looking for a professional high-integrity mortgage agent who can help you find money for your residential, commercial and construction projects, Mehdi is your go-to person in the GTA.

🌐 https://99mortgage.com/

🅕 https://www.facebook.com/99mortgage/

🅞 https://www.instagram.com/99mortgage/

🅛 https://www.linkedin.com/company/99mortgage/

Let Creativity

Boost Your Business

Amir Attar, PhD

Let Creativity Boost Your Business
Amir Attar, PhD

The undergraduate years are among the best years of your life, because they give you the opportunity and time to master any subject you focus on. Back in the day, after I passed the university entrance exam, I was faced with a choice: pursuing medicine or biology. Contrary to what the majority may have done, I chose to major in biology, for personal reasons.

I started working in my field as early as my second semester, because I believed by doing so, I could be a skilled and experienced individual once I finished my bachelor's, ready to hit the ground running. I wholeheartedly believed one is not able to gain much from theoretical studies alone, and hands-on experience is essential if you want to truly learn something. I started to work in the field of animal agriculture, working with a range of animals, from cattle to poultry. At one of my jobs, I even learned to breed the common quail. That was how I managed to earn a living over the course of my undergraduate years.

Jumping into Opportunities Feet First

When I started my master's, I had a good-hearted professor who was incredibly supportive toward me. One day, a man who had recently started a factory in the feed technology industry showed up to ask for my professor's advice and assistance. He wanted to be introduced to an expert who could help him set up and expand his factory properly. My professor referred him to me. Even though the factory was located in another town, I willingly took the offer and started to work there. Feed technology was a new field back then, and there were few people who specialized in it. That job helped me gradually become well-versed in various aspects of an emerging industry.

After three years, I decided I could offer advice to the other factories active in the field. Thus, I embarked on my new career path: feed technology consulting. After a while, as I gained more and more clients, I came to realize that I had to create systems for my work. I felt the need for a shift from the personal, independent way of doing business to a more professional, disciplined one. This gave me motivation to take my career to the next level. I decided to start a consulting firm, one whose business model was very different from the solo-consultant tradition that was common at the time. I was among the first to establish an actual consulting firm in my field. Others soon followed suit, but it was not a matter of concern for me, for I believe what matters is to be the first mover. Leaders almost always grab a great portion of market share.

Little by little, my team and I expanded our business all over the country. One of our creative innovations at the time was establishing an R&D (research and development) department to collect and screen technical material, which was regularly published and distributed as state-of-the-art scientific content on feed technology. Back then, our equipment was extremely limited compared to what we have today. There was no social media, and publishing content was not as easy as it is today. So, we used our website, fax machines and text messages to reach our audience.

One thing that kept me going was my belief in environmental determinism. I was born and raised in Mashhad, Iran, which is a big province, but not one with the best opportunities, especially in comparison to the capital. That was why I decided to do something through my work to increase Mashhad's nationwide prominence in the field of feed technology. Time passed, and we became the "name of the game" in the feed technology industry. Today, lots of big names in the industry benefit from the advice we offer.

From Consultant to Manufacturer

A while later, following another creative spark, I thought to myself, "We are leading others in our field, helping them design production lines, and advising them regarding various operational and managerial aspects, yet we are not paid what we're worth." I realized there was good money to be made in being the supplier of raw material for feed mills. Therefore, we started manufacturing supplies through partnerships with other manufacturers already in the field. We then sold what we made to other factories.

We started out ambitiously, purchased a lot of material and sold it to another organization through a deal we naively thought was a sound one. It wasn't. The buyer did not pay us for the material we gave them, in trust. We were defrauded of a large sum of money, and we found ourselves far behind square one. The fraud resulted in much trouble for me at the time, and it took almost three years to get back on my feet. Yet, I believed if one's true intention is to pay one's debts, troubles will eventually clear. So, through difficult negotiation and really hard work, I managed to pay off our debts. I didn't share the problems I was facing with my family, because I didn't want to make them unduly concerned. I thought they would hinder my progress and not let me take risks anymore.

When all was good again, I decided to establish my own factory. This time, I aimed to make my country a prominent player in feed technology in the world. However, selling products proved to be more difficult than expected. The market was filled with competitors who were intentionally giving us a hard time so they could protect their market share. This issue particularly concerned getting the necessary permits.

One day, I went to the Veterinary Organization in my city to do one more follow-up to secure the permits. This time, the man in charge made it crystal clear there was no hope. He firmly rejected my last request. I left the building in despair, and raised my head towards the sky, talking to God: "It's OK. Probably, it's not meant to be."

Right then and there, one of my staff called me on the phone, letting me know that a big-time authority had requested to talk to us. Apparently, he was visiting factories throughout the country to listen to the problems of manufacturers to ascertain if there was anything to be done to make life and business easier for them.

I wasn't in a good mood that day, yet I decided to attend the meeting. Interestingly, the authority figure took a liking to me. We talked for hours, and he finally made arrangements for our permits to come through. It was on that day that I felt the presence of God in my life. I now know God's help will show up at the most unexpected times in one's life.

We are now recognized for distinguished work in our industry, known and respected by our peers on the international scene, and

I have been recognized frequently as a leader in feed technology at international conferences and seminars. We are now expanding our business and aiming for the moon.

Creativity Matters

Creativity is a critical asset that can contribute greatly to your success. Why does creativity matter? Because it makes you think of solutions your competitors have not yet considered. It can also help you make up for what you may lack. An example that encourages creativity is the Idea Box we have set up in our company. Employees who have an innovative idea share it with us by slipping it in the box. If it is a good one, we work on it together with the person who first proposed the idea. The individual is also rewarded for their participation.

Another example is our way of creating content through a special-ized podcast we produce on feed technology. Instead of spending large amounts of money on billboards or TV commercials, this rather inexpensive method is contributing to our visibility to a noticeable degree. Remember, creativity is embedded in our nature. All we have to do is prepare the ground so it can manifest.

Now, you may ask me how a person can become more creative. One answer is to discover your own *moments*. For me, it's as simple as taking a shower. Whenever I take a shower, new ideas fill my head. For some of my friends, a short trip or a walk in nature does the job. A friend of mine, named Saeed, has his creative moments sitting in a cafe.

I would like to share with you two key concepts here: Creativity doesn't necessarily come from hard laborious work. A lot of times we get creative insights in moments of relaxation or while we're taking time off work on vacation. Secondly, I highly recommend you implement your utmost creativity on your most precious asset, your life, let's say by engaging in creative entertainment.

Right now, we are expanding our factory with a one-of-a-kind atmosphere in mind. The new design will have a cafe, a playground for children, a lobby, and many other features that separate it from a common industrial environment, which is usually quite dull and serious.

The second way to boost your creativity is to have a great partner. One place you may find a great companion is among your peers. If you are a student, you can find such a person among your classmates. All along, I have had the good fortune of having a great partner, named Reza, since my undergraduate years, an exemplary companion with whom I can share my responsibilities and work efficiently. If you are on your own, being overwhelmed with too many tasks may inhibit your creativity. In my case, since my partner and I share responsibilities, we have more time on our hands to be creative, thus able to work on novel ideas and enjoy continuous growth.

The third way is to take the time to investigate different pathways that could lead to success. For example, a while ago, we decided we didn't want to be limited to manufac-turing. We were considering starting other businesses in our industry, one of which was importing and exporting feed additives and animal feed products. Another was to produce raw materials for poultry and livestock mineral supplements. Yet, because we did not have the time and capacity, we thought of partnering with a number of experts who could help us achieve this goal. We did exactly that. Thankfully, the business has taken off, and we are doing great. I believe you don't need to start everything from scratch or do everything all by yourself. You can use other people's skills and abilities to expand your horizons.

This year, at the time of writing this book, we have experienced lots of problems due to insufficient financing and troubles with supplying raw material, so I acted creatively and managed to form more intimate relationships with my suppliers. Over time, I sent them gifts as a gesture of goodwill, and I managed to purchase from them our required raw material at a reasonable price and in large volumes. Thus, we prevented the dire situation of being forced to buy at higher prices or running into possible shortages.

In summary, I believe creativity, when supported by effort and hard work, can help you attain your goals and see your wishes fulfilled. Creativity is not a big word. It could apply to the smallest tasks of everyday life: You can try a new breakfast. You can send creative gifts to your customers. You can think of innovative ways to engage potential new customers.

Now, if you believe in creativity, you need to hire creative people. How can you do that? One way is to use standardized tests, available in the market, that measure the creativity of an individual. And that's not all. After the recruitment of the right individual, if you want true creativity to prevail in your organization, *you* must now be the creative leader, a role model for your staff. Otherwise, your employees' creative potential will remain untapped.

I would like to wrap up this chapter by sharing a nugget of wisdom with any young readers. Start working as soon as you can, no later than getting your bachelor's degree. In my opinion, solely studying and pursuing higher education won't help if you don't apply theories in practice. Try to work a few years between undergraduate and graduate years, either by setting up your own business or working for others. Personally, I didn't start my PhD until I had worked in the field for several years. Actually, I promised myself I wouldn't even take the PhD entrance exam unless I could drive to the test location in my own great car. And I did. I am especially grateful for having a kind supportive professor during my PhD years. It was such a blessing.

Let Creativity
Boost Your Business

Author's Bio

Khorak Pardaz Hazareh Novin Co. was established by **Amir Attar** and his partner, Reza, in 2008 with the aim of providing organized consultation in the livestock and poultry feed industry.

At first, all the company's revenues came from its scientific services, including formulation, designing production lines, holding seminars, etc. About two years after the company's establishment, Amir and Reza decided to produce certain products based on the latest scientific findings. They also conducted a need assessment in the livestock and poultry feed industry, so that scientific and the pragmatic information would give rise to a solid foundation for production. Yet, due to a number of financial issues and lack of a production line, manufacturing of these products was put into action through paid partnership with other factories.

About four years after the company was founded, they rented a facility and set up a simple production line. They then produced their products, sold them, and soon decided to build a factory of their own.

Today, Khorak Pardaz Hazareh Novin Co., using the latest technology and a very beautiful and unique design, is one of the world-class factories in the production of nutrition supplements and concentrates for livestock, poultry and aquaculture.

Amir holds a PhD in poultry nutrition and is the CEO of Khorak Pardaz Hazareh Novin Co. He has written extensively on feed technology and is the founder of the feed technology website http://en.nmfeed.com/. He is the editor of the journal *Feed Processing Science* and has published numerous papers on animal feed in the world's most prestigious journals. He is also a well-known speaker in the field of feed technology.

Contact Amir at:

✉ amirattar58@yahoo.com;

🌐 info@nmfeed.com;

📞 +985136578234-6

The Threshold of
Bliss

Solmaz Barghgir

The Threshold of Bliss

Solmaz Barghgir

Deeply anxious and stressed, I felt all my hopes verging on collapse when I finally made up my mind. After failing in a serious relationship for the second time, I called off my wedding. Images of my friends and family passed before my eyes, and I kept thinking about the countless rebukes awaiting me. However, I had decided to bring that phase of my life to an end. I would start over again, as I often did throughout my life.

The Beginning of an End

When I chose to end my first marriage, my family had already immigrated to Canada. The divorce put an end to an unhappy eight years of my life, but it also left me alone. I knew I needed to start afresh and move in a new direction, so I immersed myself in everything I could think of, including attending courses on Jungian psychology and enrolling in self-development classes. I also travelled around the country and met people from all walks of life.

Loneliness presented a painful challenge for me during this time. I ultimately decided on moving to Canada to live with my family. My lawyer told me the immigration process could take at most three years, so I began making plans based on the assumption that I would stay in Iran for that length of time.

I gave up on my graduate studies because I believed I would not have enough time to finish them. I was living without my family in an environment where, as a woman, my identity only existed as a part of that family. I did not prefer to lie about my life and my personal situation, but in my daily interactions, I had no choice but to hide the truth from inquisitive strangers.

I felt lost. Since I struggled to feel invested in any of my jobs, I changed career paths regularly. I left my position as a quality manager, which I previously held for over five years. Later, I entered the marketing field and worked as a sales manager for a while. In virtually all of my interactions, whether they involved personal relationships or people I met at work, I chose to lie about parts of my life to gain approval. If I went to an interview, the manager would ask me all kinds of questions, including many of an entirely personal nature, not pertaining to the job. In Iran, the concept of privacy does not possess the same meaning it does in Canada and asking such questions did not constitute an invasion of privacy. In fact, many Iranians do not generally concern themselves with concepts like the invasion of privacy. Expectation therefore dictated that I explain all sorts of personal matters.

After just emerging from a long and destructive relationship, trusting other people proved rather challenging. In an attempt to put as much distance as possible between myself and my former life, I cut ties with most of the friends that I met through my ex-husband. In my personal life, as well as professionally, I did not want others to know about my past or to judge me for my current situation.

I did not fare much better regarding my love life, either. As soon as my dates learned about my immigrant application process, everything turned upside down. They would start acting strangely, and I noticed that my interests ceased to be important in those relationships. Each of these prospective partners became fixated on finding a way to use our relationship to pave the way for his own immigration. To be fair, not all of the men I met acted this way; however, once I recognized that a couple of them only maintained interest in me for this particular reason, my trust issue grew even worse.

The Winds of Change

At a certain point, I met someone who seemed different from the rest. After studying to work as a medical doctor, he turned down a neurosurgery residency to start his own business because he considered the latter to be a much more lucrative option. I would describe him as a genius in the true sense of the word, as well as a true gentleman. He consistently showed all kinds of consideration in our romantic relationship and possessed all the traits I had learned to admire in a man. Basically, he represented an updated version of my own father: a man with strict self-discipline and a man with a plan. One might say that he had it all: the looks, the money, the great family, and the travel experience. To top it all off, he did not need to use me to get to Canada; he had already applied to take that step before we met.

I felt the winds of change starting to blow. I introduced him to my family, and he remarkably succeeded in earning my parents' approval – no easy feat. I had spent my entire life searching for ways to receive the same level of approval from them. When we travelled to Canada together to meet my family, not only my strict mother, but also my sisters, approved of my new partner. I could hardly believe it!

He and I chose to return to Iran and get married while await-ing the completion of his immigration process. Over time, I had progressed into a great position along my career path. At this point, I worked for a German company in Iran and even earned a promotion to the regional office in Dubai. I prepared myself to give all of it up to marry this man and build a new life with him in Canada.

"Fail again; fail better."[1]

Unfortunately, I struggled with a strange feeling that my love life seemed too good to be true. A voice inside me kept suggest-ing that something felt wrong. On the surface, we were a happy couple. I always focussed on his positive characteristics. Nonetheless, whenever I was alone with my own thoughts, something bothered me.

I became convinced that I was not his top priority. His top priority was his mother. As I said, he was a very clever man, and it took me a while to distinguish his unbreakable bond with his mom. At the same time, while he had met and liked me just the way I was, complete with all my positive and negative traits, now and then, he would find a subtle way to change me to adopt the ways he preferred.

One day my fiancé called and, in a faltering voice, told me his parents had just found out about my first marriage. I was shocked, because I assumed they had known all along, but he said he had

---

1 Samuel Beckett

never told them. He asked for some time to "sort things out." This development happened a few weeks before our wedding. He said he was sure his parents would come around.

A week passed. I started to realize that, in this relationship, like all the previous important decisions in my life, I had been looking for other people's approval. What I liked about this man was his image in the eyes of others, his money, and his acceptance by my parents. It was now clear to me I was not his top priority. I decided this was not the kind of life I wanted for myself.

This was the beginning of a major change in my mindset, a paradigm shift which changed everything for me.

I called my best friend and asked her to cancel the wedding plans. She begged me to reconsider, saying I was throwing away my chance at happiness. He had so many positive points, she pleaded, and I should not let this small shortcoming ruin everything. I told her that my entire future happiness pivoted on that "small shortcoming," and I could not wager everything on someone when I was not that person's top priority. I told her I had made up my mind, and I had to give up this marriage if I ever wanted to be happy.

I remember very well the night I told my family about my decision. I felt miserable. I did not want them to change my mind, so I only told them after my friend had actually canceled the wedding. As I told them the news, my eyes welled up. They could not believe what they were hearing and tried to change my mind, but I held my ground and told them the decision had already been made.

Revaluation Time

While I was in the process of making my decision, I made a list of the pros and cons I had experienced in that relationship. It was only then I realized everything I liked about him was because I wanted to gain others' approval. I realized his being rich or his being a doctor were not things that made me happy. I just wanted other people to see what a rich and educated husband I had. We would stay at 5-star hotels when we travelled around the world. Of course, I liked that. I enjoyed it immensely, but was that really a priority for me? Absolutely not! Sometime later, when I told him about my list of pros and cons, he refused to believe me, saying, "Of course, my being rich and educated is important to you. Everybody cares about stuff like that."

But he was wrong, and I proved I did not care about those trivial matters with my eventual marriage. This time, I decided I would not let other people's opinions influence my decision. There was only one question I posed to myself: Can I take responsibility for the decisions that would make me happy, or not?

I had given up my job in Iran, and it was time to build a new life in a completely new environment I knew next to nothing about. Initially, I resumed my original job as a quality manager, but after a while, I realized that role was not making me happy. I sat down and made a list of things that did make me happy. I wanted to help people. I wanted to dress up for work every day. I wanted to socialize a lot to get to know the people in this new country. Finally, I settled on employment in a bank. I still have the paper on which I had made this list. It holds a place of honour in my office.

My quality of life had declined in many ways. I had just left the country of my youth. Almost all of my close friends were back home. I needed to build my professional career from scratch. I had to work hard to be eligible for the funds and grants I needed for my studies to further my career. And it was all worth it in the end.

Light at the End of the Tunnel

Eventually, I started dating again, but this time around, I prioritized myself rather than other people. Over time, I studied in "Tony Robbins Coaching School" and became a "Relationship Coach". I am now happily married to a wonderful Canadian man and we have a son.

The truth is I have everything I always wanted. All this was possible only because I stopped allowing other people's desires for my life to dominate my own true priorities, and I started choosing and doing what I want to do with my life. I focus on what makes me happy when I face important decisions in my life.

We have all heard the saying that we live only once, but how many of us live our lives as if we only have one chance at realizing our dreams. I have come to know that I am the one who will enjoy my life, and I am the one who should take responsibility for it. I am the one who must be ready to live with the consequences of my decisions.

The threshold of bliss is found when you consciously and conscientiously accept the implications of your decisions. I got the chance to understand truly the importance of this fact in my life. When we put ourselves in uncomfortable and miserable situations, just to appease others, the pain we force on our minds, hearts and bodies is highly destructive. Living this way can devastate us.

There is nothing wrong with seeking other people's approval, as long as you can live with the consequences and take responsibility for those consequences. Beware that regret might ensue, because that particular decision might lead to your personal unhappiness.

What if those same people whose approval you sought decide to change their minds? This, in fact, is the most important life lesson. I should know what my intentions are, and to what extent other people's opinions influence my decisions. If I allow others' opinions to influence my decision, am I ready to live with the consequences?

Sometimes, clear warning signs are present, but we refuse to acknowledge them. We might be caught in the moment and fail to see them. Eventually, we will face the consequences of our choices. We were born to be happy. Seeking others' approval and acquiescing to their ever-changing whims will inevitably lead to unhappiness. True happiness doesn't come from what others demand of you. It flows from your efforts to move towards your heart's desires.

The Threshold of Bliss

Author's Bio

As an Effective Relationship Strategist, Solmaz Barghgir empowers individuals to express themselves courageously to boost their professional performance and personal relationships. Solmaz helps her clients adopt a growth mindset, see failures as opportunities, and set realistic goals and plan towards achieving them through a personalized strategy.

Solmaz's unique background has prepared her in better understanding her clients' needs. Growing up in Iran, her family helped create supportive and healthy environments for underprivileged children. With her abilities of caring for others and seeing the potential in everyone, she is a champion of creating supportive circles; be it for women in shelters with serious relationship problems; or for those new to the workforce needing to align themselves with their new country's culture and norms.

Solmaz runs her coaching practice in Toronto, "Powerful Life Coaching". She continues to be a student of her own personal development. Solmaz has over 15 years of study in the form of many books and workshops, and she is a proud graduate of two world-renowned institutions: Psychoanalysis Training Program - CG Jung-Institute and the Robbins-Madanes Life Coaching School. She is a Distinguished Toastmaster, a motivational speaker and has taken on many leadership roles for Toastmaters International.

Solmaz sees growth as a flower that needs all the right elements to thrive. As an "Effective Relationship Strategist", she enables clients to cultivate meaningful personal and professional relationships to bring their goals to fruition.

Solmaz is a proud mom to her precious son Darian and, in her free time, she enjoys being one with nature and making time for self-reflection.

Connect with her at:

🌐 www.barghgir.com.

Integrity

Is Key to Flourishing

Lino Contento

Integrity Is Key to Flourishing
Lino Contento

Over the course of the years I've worked in the banking industry, there are stories that leave an impression on you. Ones you can't forget, and people's/families' lives you helped change forever. This is the reason why I work so hard and love what I do. One Story that continues to stay with me is of a couple who needed the help of a professional experienced mortgage advisor. On paper, based on their financial status and self employment, this couple was not qualified for the kind of mortgage they needed based on standard lending criteria. Only an experienced mortgage professional would be able to help them with the solutions and appropriate program that could secure them their much-needed mortgage, without presenting the bank with false and made-up documents which is what a mortgage broker had advised them to do.

The couple was introduced to me by their realtor. The realtor, a friend of mine and long-time realtor referral source, heard about their not-so-honest mortgage broker, who wanted to charge a hefty $15,000 fee in order to secure a mortgage for them. The realtor regarded this as sheer insanity, and he decided to refer the couple to me for a second opinion.

When I heard about the situation in which this couple found themself in, whose selfish intentions were not completely unfamiliar to me (one could not believe how many times this type of case occurs), I was determined to correct the wrong. In fact,

I have always attempted to stick to my values of integrity and honesty. The couple was surprised to learn I wasn't going to charge them for the same service. With me, there was no fee at all. None. This is what happens when you work with a Mortgage Specialist from a bank, you receive expert advice without any fees or strings attached.

I was happy when the couple eventually managed to get what they wanted. I became the hero of their story because I helped them save a lot of money, helped get them into their dream home. And *this* is what makes my work fulfilling.

Integrity Keeps Me in the Game

I have worked with RBC (Royal Bank of Canada) since 1996. Over the years, a lot of people have entered my industry and my line of work. Yet, most come and go, and I have remained. The key to my kind of sustainability is integrity. When it comes to my business, integrity is of the utmost importance.

It is sometimes unclear to people why integrity matters in a field where money is the most important word. I believe when you set out to help someone get the kind of mortgage they want, you should have a long-term frame of mind. Yes, I do want to make money for what I am good at, but at what cost? I am not doing anybody any good if, for example, I help you get a mortgage whose payments you are not able to handle. In a few years, you would lose the house, and everybody would then point a finger at me as the person who helped you get into a home that was way over your head. The short-minded financial advisor, who goes to the ends of the earth to close such a deal, knowing that you won't be able to afford the payments, should give a reality-check to their underlying intentions. Integrity, as I always advise the up-and-comers in the business, is key.

In addition to understanding the centrality of integrity to flourishing in this business, one might also need to understand how to integrate integrity into the day-to-day work processes. I believe that creating a habit of finding an honest alternative will do the job.

For instance, imagine that you needed a mortgage to buy a house, but all the revenue you generate in your household, stated income and otherwise, is not sufficient to be approved for the mortgage. One way that some mortgage agents can help you, is to create the kind of paperwork that gets you the loan, no matter what the consequences are for you. After all, they have the experience and can easily create the illusion for the bank that you are a fit candidate for the loan. However, what then happens to you? You'll lose the house at some point in the future because you can't afford the payments. Not today. Not tomorrow. But eventually you would lose your home. So, I will stick to the integrity principle and see how we can come up with a better solution. Perhaps, together, we would come to realize that an alternative would be to share the liability between you and your brother. The two incomes put together would help you get approved, and you can rest assured that nobody is going to lose a house. I would be doing right by you, the bank, the government and society at large.

Another essential piece of advice to keep in mind is that integrity is a mutual bond. It's not always the advisor who might be the "bad guy." Take the case of the family of four who approached me to help them secure a mortgage for a one-million-dollar house. The parents had falsely claimed they lived separately so they would receive two separate welfare checks. All members of the family had an income, and their combined earnings added up to the amount they needed for the payments. The mortgage would be paid off, they could happily live in the house without the fear of losing it, I would benefit from a handsome commission, the bank would profit from the deal, and no *fraud, per se*, was involved. However, as an insider, I knew that most of their income wasn't honest. It wasn't an honest deal. Therefore, I refused to take them on as clients.

Cases such as this demand that you be on the extreme end of the integrity spectrum. Most of the time, people such as the ones in this story will come back to you to show they managed to do it without you. They go and find someone else to get the job done. I believe you should not necessarily be the hero of everyone's story.

Integrity as a Family Value

When I was younger, my father always told me: "Integrity and honesty keep the worries of life at bay." If you work with integrity, you don't need to worry about the bank, or the tax guys, or the government, or anybody else figuring out what you did. Your records are clear. You are known for your honesty. And people keep coming back to you. This is the true sense of sustainability in business. My father's words are what I would put on a billboard for everybody to see every day.

A Final Thought

In addition to integrity, I have another morsel of wisdom to share: Make it about the people, the clients. Whatever you give to the world, you will find it coming back to you ten-fold. This has been my personal experience. For instance, one of my guiding principles has always been to establish a friendship with my clients. People need a go-to expert, not just for the advice they offer, but also for the friendship they provide. People prefer to work with someone who has integrity and is caring at the same time.

I always get to know my clients and ask about their lives, not in an intrusive manner, but in a friendly way. I ask about their spouse, their children, their job, their health issues. I bond with them. This is how I manage to figure out if they need help other than the kind of advice they come to me for. And I willingly help them when I spot the need and see that the solution is within my power to connect the dots.

Friendship is among the best things you can give the world. For example, if you asked me to introduce you to an auto dealer, choosing between my friend and Tom, who is the greatest auto dealer in the region, I would refer you to my friend. After all, he's my friend. I know him. I know his wife. His children. I know about his back problem.

It's not just these universal factors that contribute to one's success. There are also people and things in your personal life which are part of that formula. For me, for example, my wife has been the greatest influence in my success. She has been my partner since 2009. I was successful before her, but success became a part of every single dimension of my life ever since she entered my life. Striking a balance between work and home, which can be the greatest challenge of all businesspeople, has become no challenge for me, thanks to her and her contributions to our family and business.

Integrity Is Key to Flourishing

Author's Bio

Lino Contento has worked in the banking industry since 1987. He has been with RBC since 1996 and a Mortgage Specialist since 2001. He is Multiple Sales Conference Award winner, Chairman's Round Table winner, Platinum/Gold Club winner and is ranked in the top 1% across Canada for RBC. Lino is a Star Convention Recipient and winner of 3 Leo Awards.

Buying a home is a major decision. Whether you've just started your research or are actively house-hunting, Lino can help provide you with the personalized advice and solutions you need to make your home ownership goals happen. Whether it's getting your first mortgage, refinancing or moving your mortgage to RBC, he can help! Lino will work with you to ensure your financing suits both your current and future needs. You can feel confident you're working with an expert who has your best interests in mind.

Lino specializes in helping:

- First-time home buyers
- Switching/Refinancing your mortgage to RBC
- New to Canada mortgages
- Foreign income mortgages
- Self-employed mortgages

Lino has six children and is happily married to his wife/partner Danielle Palazzo, also an RBC Mortgage Specialist And award winner.

Contact him at:

📞 (905) 553-3270.

You can also find him on Facebook, Instagram and LinkedIn.

Racquet Rules
That Defined My Life

Sina Dejnabadi

Racquet Rules That Defined My Life

Sina Dejnabadi

"What I think I've been able to do well over the years is play with pain, play with problems, play in all sorts of conditions."
- Roger Federer

At the age of eighteen, as I entered university, I decided to become financially self-reliant. Since then, my career has been full of highs and lows. I have had considerable achievements as somebody who started with nothing but succeeded through hard work and consistent effort. Of course, I have experienced major failures too, failures that could knock one out of the way completely, with no chance of recovery.

I started in a British firm as a computer maintainer and operator of an Excel-like software named Lotus, working for only $19 a month. I observed carefully what was happening around me, closely watching the executives of companies like Bosch and General Electrics GE, which we represented, as they came and went. I kept in mind the way they dressed, the way they talked, and their body language.

I observed serious people with big hearts and others who were weak and cowardly. I was determined to pick one group as role models, choosing between "moderation and comfort" and "tending to fly high with all the challenges."

In 2002, I was faced with the first big decision of my life: to embark on a personal business venture with my father or keep working for my employer of six years.

The former came with little initial income and tremendous responsibilities, a high-risk journey. So, at that crossroads, I opted to keep my secure job. I stuck with the comfort of higher wages, a personal driver, and beautiful offices in fancy neighborhoods. Nonetheless, I felt like I was successful while constrained to a cage. My team and I posted a five-year sales record of nearly $85 million in the oil and gas industry from 2004-2009. I was earning a great income every single month. Anybody would have been pleased with that situation, but for me, it was like missing out on the opportunity to rise further.

I first held a racquet in my hand and stepped onto a tennis court in 2007. At the time, I worked very hard 24/7, and I was desperately looking for a way to interrupt the work-dominated tone of my life at the age of 29. Even during my time on the court, when the coach was teaching me the rules or the name of the strokes, or when I was practicing the moves, I was thinking about my job. I evoked images and made patterns in my mind. I never became a decent tennis player, but through learning the rules and the spirit of the sport, I discovered precious principles, which made me stronger, more flexible, and more optimistic.

The following rules I adopted playing tennis and applied elsewhere where they worked for me:

Rule No.1: You are not invincible, even if you are the champion of the world.

We have all seen multiple Grand Slam champions being stunned by unheralded opponents in lower-tier tournaments. When I first started my own business as a twenty-year-old, it was a total failure and I was forced to retreat. In 2002, I made another poor decision by choosing to remain an employee instead of starting my own business. Then in 2010, I finally embarked on a journey as an entrepreneur. And in 2011, just when I felt like the happiest man on the planet, having my own enterprise, my life was torn apart. I thought I had become the champion, but while I was carried away by the achievement, I suffered an unbelievably severe defeat. My wife decided to file for divorce after ten years of marriage. Nonetheless, I still had the choice to remain a failure or learn the lessons and rise again. I said to myself: "You will never become a champion if you give up after a single defeat."

I was hit by another failure in 2012, when a supplier of my company caused me to incur a loss of $150,000 by not fulfilling its commitments in an oil and gas project. In 2014, just when I was bouncing back again, an investor I knew in China agreed to fund $600,000 in my Canadian company within three years in exchange for a share in the business. I was on a high, pouring in all my money, until my new partner ended up in prison, and all the assets and the contract were gone. Again, I had to make a decision. Should I let go of the racquet and leave the court or, instead, lace up my sneakers and keep practicing? I went with the latter choice.

Rule No. 2: You'll definitely lose if you believe you are the inferior.

It doesn't matter against whom you are playing. You will surely lose the game if you believe in your own failure. That's why I took so many risks, which turned out to be big-time crashes as well as major achievements.

Back in 2004, a client was looking for a supplier in a massive oil project. I didn't know the project manager, but I had heard he had a disappointing record of previous collaboration with my colleagues, as well as my boss, which was why he did not answer any of our phone calls.

I told my boss of my intention to get involved in the project. He utterly refused my offer, as he asserted: "The guy will never work with us." I asked him for a chance, and he reluctantly accepted. I called the project manager, not once but on six different occasions, and each time he rejected me. I asked him to meet with me for only half an hour. I was determined to land the contract. All my efforts eventually paid off, as I managed to persuade the client. I listened to what he had to say and told him that I understood his skepticism. I simply asked him to give me a chance without any further commitment.

My team and I worked tirelessly while we stayed confident about this victory. Just a couple of months later, our new client and I signed a $1.8 million contract in Milan, which turned out to be one of the sweetest achievements of my career.

Rule No. 3: If you're not in the right position, the ball either hits you or moves past you.

When my trainer told me about this rule for the first time, I immediately remembered all the awkward situations in my life and career with which I hadn't been ready to deal. Most of the time, you must be prepared for a challenge, acquire the necessary knowledge, do in-depth research, or simply gear up for a meeting. The ball hit me squarely in the face every time I wasn't well prepared. In 2020, when the world was ravaged by the coronavirus, those who were not prepared, and those who were not cautious enough, lost their jobs and businesses. Many people lost their relationships, just because they were not aware of the hazard coming their way. My coaches and the other role models I have had in life taught me to make the best of any crisis. Covid-19 presented an opportunity to thrive, a chance to rebuild. That's when I started to do things that would contribute to my success, things I wouldn't have been choosing under normal circumstances.

Rule No. 4: Stronger opponents improve your skills.

Tennis is a unique sport, because a player plays a more fascinating game against a stronger opponent. Playing against an average opponent will keep you from delivering your best performance. If you want to become top-notch, you have no choice but to take on great players. Triumphs over lesser competitors might bring you trophies, but they will definitely not be the ones to remember.

When you listen to wise people, you can improve yourself. They can teach you how to learn from your failures and how to behave under trying circumstances. They'll show you how to recover from a setback, taking responsibility, rather than looking for a scapegoat. Inferior people may have the opposite effects. I've always chosen to listen to multiple opinions, but I only cherry-pick the encouraging comments. Outstanding individuals can push you forward because they know the game inside and out. Weak people bring up fears and failures. They'll make you lose sleep over making an investment. Strong characters won't let you surrender, offering you clues to bounce back, even when they're confident you're the one to blame.

When I was offered positions at companies such as GE and Bosch, I found the self-esteem to square off against bigger players at high-profile occasions. Million-dollar projects became feasible for me.

Following this advice, you won't have to be anxious about financial crashes. You'll be able to feel positive about having ambitious goals in order to achieve success.

Rule No. 5: Doubles play on a wider court.

There are two lines bordering the sides of a tennis court. These two areas, called doubles alley, don't count in singles matches, only coming into play when you're playing two on two. What I've learned from years of experience is that a duo will always perform better than one. Carrying the entire burden on your own shoulders is not the best tactic. I owe the $85 million sale in the oil and gas business to a committed, devoted, and energetic team of colleagues. There were times I was fooled by the idea of single-handedly getting the job done, and each time, I hit a brick wall or failed to accomplish my primary objective. It's through teamwork that people support each other, share ideas and offer clues to one another. A trustworthy team becomes like family. They can pull you up and, in the low times, they're the ones that encourage you to bounce back.

Between 2014 and 2017, my sister Sara and I dealt with all aspects of our business. We received products at our warehouse, sorted them, packaged orders, did the marketing, visited our clients, and met with suppliers. But one day, we appointed a well-experienced warehousing company, named JBK, to manage the inventory and logistics. A team of experts in content production, managed by my wife Sherry, took charge of our social media. And we hired a professional group of editors to produce instructional videos for online training purposes.

We probably posted lower profit in each area, but significant business growth saw the overall earnings rise threefold. I learned that it takes a skillful team to run a successful Instagram page for e-commerce. If someone tells me one day that "uploading some posts and hashtags is not such a big deal," I would say he or she is playing on a small court, not thinking big enough.

Rule No. 6: The serve is the most crucial stroke.

For a lot of reasons, the serve is the most important shot in tennis. As you toss the ball in the air you need to make several simultaneous movements before you hit it with the racquet. It is crucial that the ball is thrown right above your head, and at the same time, your racquet whips up and around before you take a well-timed shot with a proper angle. The aim of your ball is a small rectangular area in the opponent's half, and besides all that, you have to be careful with the power of the shot and the bending of your knees as you lean backward to hit the serve.

We so often lose our concentration when faced with complications in life that require us to move in various directions all at once, making key decisions. That's when we have to make the appropriate moves. We need to be flexible, just like the body of a tennis player. We need to act quickly before we lose an opportunity, just like an accomplished player whose opponent doesn't even have the chance to see the ball.

Rule No. 7: If you want to succeed in tennis, don't over-think.

Your opponent's ball could land anywhere in your half of the court. You might have to move toward the net or reach the baseline for a return shot. While you're moving, you will have to set the proper position for your hand, body, and the racquet before hitting the ball. A professional player does all that so deftly, without overthinking, in less than a second. It takes years of preparation to acquire that skill, playing as if being on autopilot mode. Hard work and practice instill a treasure of non-deliberate movements into a professional player, so that he or she makes a routine of taking accurate strokes.

I survived through failures in my career and elsewhere in my life with a simple assumption: There is no disaster as long as I stay alive, as there's always a chance to start again and achieve even more.

Rule No. 8: You need a coach, even as a champion. All the best players are schooled by top coaches and mentors, on and off the court. Players look their coaches in the eye, whether in victory or defeat, and gain energy from them. Technique, support, and motivation are what an outstanding trainer can offer. Every time I was frustrated by a collapse, I was privileged to take time with international coaches and mentors in order to thrive, both personally and professionally. They helped me listen carefully to questions and come up with proper answers. They taught me how to tackle my weak spots, be upbeat about my skills, and get back in the game stronger. An inspiring coach, in whom you trust and with whom you feel comfortable, is the most precious asset you can have in the face of adversity. A master helps you achieve all you seek: money, a new opportunity, etc.

Tennis was much more than a sporting activity or just a simple diversion for me. It's been years since I played the game on a court, but every time I look at my tennis bag, I recall all those valuable lessons that filled me with the aspiration to move forward and succeed.

Racquet Rules That Defined My Life

Author's Bio

Sina Dejnabadi is a best-selling author, entrepreneur, business coach, industrial engineer, as well as a certified international business specialist in Canada. Sina is an elite member of Forum for Canada's International Trade Training, known as FITT. Sina is a qualified expert in interior decoration as well as an NLP and Timeline Therapy Practitioner.

Sina is the President and CEO of Samia Canada Inc, the number one supplier of honeycomb panels in Canada. He also owns an E-commerce, online retail, social media and digital marketing agency called Samicore. Moreover, Sina is the founder of a coaching platform named as First Class Seat Coaching in which he gives his audience consultancy on their personal and professional lives.

Sina's career life began back in 1996. As a very young man, who had decided to realise his dream, he started his quest and he soon saw himself gaining a wealth of experience in a variety of areas. In his journey, which has continued to date, Sina has made tremendous achievements in a wide range of fields, including oil, gas, petrochemicals, quality assurance, ISO standards, constrution, interior design, international business, as well as e-commerce and social media marketing. In a period of 24 years, Sina was significantly active in projects conducted by more than 20 European and multinational companies, including General Electrics (GE), Saint Gobain, Bosch Rexroth, and more. Sina thinks of his experiences as "his greatest achievement."

His expertise in NLP and Timeline Therapy, together with trainings given to him by the greatest coaches in the world, are among the very reasons why his clients can trust him. He has already life- and business-coached more than 200 people throughout their journeys in their personal and professional lives.

Should you wish to contact Sina and his team as well as check out his products and training courses, you can reach him at:

🌐 www.sina1shot.com.

(You can reach all his professional websites, contacts, emails and social media page at the above link.)

Do Not Ask How.

Ask Why.

Dr. Kevin Engel

Do Not Ask How. Ask Why.

Dr. Kevin Engel

Fear of a Sudden Ending

The thought of death can make an individual change the trajectory of their life. I possess a deeply personal understanding of this concept because cancer runs through generations in my family. At some point, the fear of being diagnosed with a terminal disease sets in, and all of a sudden, one must plan for an uncertain future.

Almost a decade ago, my father received a cancer diagnosis. The doctor estimated that he would live a mere seven years longer.[2]

After receiving this news, my father told me, "Kevin, since I am now diagnosed with cancer, your mother had cancer, and even your sister had cancer, I guess you need to just get yourself tested to see if everything is OK."

I went to a doctor who ran some blood tests. Shockingly, they determined that my liver enzymes were abnormally high, causing me a lot of concern. Additional testing revealed a spot on my shoulder, which raised suspicions about bone cancer. I proceeded to get some bone tests conducted, as well.

The cancer scares only marked the beginning of my stress. Suddenly, I worried about the future because I had established no source of passive income. In my profession as an optometrist, I made good money, but I essentially traded hour for

---

2 Thankfully, Dad is still alive and doing OK.

dollar. If for any reason I stopped working, no money would come in the next day.

Around the same time, another friend of mine told me about no longer being able to work full-time while she cared for her husband during his cancer treatment. My wife happens to be an optometrist, also. After hearing my friend's words, I felt alarmed by the prospect of leaving the burden of my life on my wife's shoulders. If I fell ill, she would undoubtedly need to work more and take care of more stuff. I always thought, if I couldn't work, she could support us. I realized that even though she would have done this without complaint, she would be carrying too much weight for one person. I did not want that.

A Destination with Unknown Roads

I felt inexplicable relief learning that I did not have cancer. I remember my doctor calling me fortunate because the tests found no liver cancer. When I asked why, he responded, "If it had been liver cancer, you would not be alive by now." I didn't know whether to feel happy or sad about such a grave statement.

When I began obsessing over the vulnerable future of my family's financial security, the same friend told me how critical disability insurance proved very helpful for her and her husband during their tough times. My disability insurance did not include critical disability, and in fact, the companies deemed me ineligible for this particular type of life insurance. They denied this specific coverage for a simple reason: cancer appeared throughout my family history. Once I reported that my mother, sister, and father survived cancer, no insurance company would risk that type of insurance on me. I committed myself to devise a plan to generate passive income.

Consequently, I developed a definite and clear financial goal: making $10,000 of passive income each month within the next five years. I felt if we had $10,000 a month in passive income, it would not affect our life style if I couldn't work. I needed a detailed financial plan to help me achieve this goal. The process of drawing up such a plan proved far more difficult than I initially thought.

The Paradigm Shift

At that point I started to toy with a few ideas and I shared my goal with my friends and family. One day, one of these friends told me, "Kevin, you should read this great book." He handed me Rich Dad, Poor Dad by Robert Kiyosaki and shared that he now enjoyed passive income from rental property due to inspiration gained from reading the book. As I read the book for myself, I learned its simple governing idea: changing earning mentality from working and being paid on a daily basis to working once and being paid over and over. This concept initially seemed rather foreign to me. I grew up believing that I must work hard to be paid for the work that I do. In other words, I thought, "The harder I work, the more I get paid." Though this may remain true if one wants to generate linear income, it does not apply to accruing passive income. Reading Kiyosaki's book helped tremendously to raise my financial intelligence. I learned how money is made and how assets work to generate cash flow. I found out that while owning a business can result in financial gain, going beyond that to make money residually by investing in proper opportunities holds the potential for even more. In the words of Kiyosaki, moving beyond owning a business sets the stage for making money even without working as much. According to the book, I could work on applying this concept within the real estate industry. I happened to like the real estate business process, including finding a house, fixing it up, and eventually selling it. I understood the property sections of the book very well. My father even devoted some time to a real estate business in the past, and I recalled learning a few things from him.

My second breakthrough realization was that I needed a mentor, someone to be there to show me which steps to take based on her or his experience. I wanted to work alongside someone who achieved similar goals to the one I set for myself. At this point, I turned to my father for advice, as I respect his thoughts and opinions. However, when I told him I planned to enter the real estate business, he advised me against it. After experiencing ups and downs in his own life, his views regarding the real estate industry became rather conservative. I took his advice into consideration, but I still decided to seek more viewpoints from others who had achieved success in the business.

The Sense of a Beginning

One day while eating brunch at a friend's home, I talked at length about my budding interest in real estate. I left his house with a book entitled 51 Success Stories from Canadian Real Estate Investors, written by Don R. Campbell. This book contained stories from numerous people who became successful through investing in real estate. I immediately realized with whom I could consult for advice. Without hesitation, I looked up Don R. Campbell, and the next week I attended a seminar in Edmonton where I met his group and learned of the ACRE system used to create wealth. I noticed how some people specialized in multifamily buildings, others in single-family buildings, fourplexes, duplexes, and so on. I had to not only find my own strategy, but also to determine where to start. One of the main challenges I faced in this endeavor pertained to time. As an optometrist with three children, I could reasonably invest a weekend to attend meetings and events, but I considered anything beyond that too demanding on my time. The first house I bought only required a half-hour drive from my own home, but this added up quickly when I went back and forth every time I wanted to show the house. I sold the house for a profit, but I needed to go beyond my own neighborhood. I felt overwhelmed by the thousands of places available throughout Canada where I could invest. I absolutely did not have enough time to screen every single one of them.

Gratefully, I found Peter Kinch, a mortgage broker active in the real estate business. Getting to know him benefitted my business and financial plans in major ways. When he heard about my goal, he told me exactly how to achieve it. He gave me the how I had long been seeking: If I bought six or seven fourplexes, held them for five years, then sold a few of them to cover the mortgages, I would be good to go. I executed these steps and ended up with my name in one of Canada's most prestigious real estate magazines, just eighteen short months after attending the ACRE meeting.

Blending the Vicarious and the Experienced

Finding my way to success and stability was not easy for me. I learned a lot from many people along the way. I am happy with where I am now, but I cannot deny that I faced moments of fear and loss. I feel so grateful for my many mentors, from friends who gave me reading suggestions and personal advice to experts who generously provided me with professional advice.

Here are four guidelines selected from the many I learned from experiencing the ups and downs of the business:

1. Be clear and definite about your goal. At the beginning, even though I felt intimidated by my goal, it was highly charged emotionally, and guided me through the hardships. A clear and definite goal will keep you from letting go of your aims when faced with trouble.

2. Find a mentor who currently does what you want to do, not one who did it in the past. Someone who did it twenty-five years ago probably worked with a different system. Track down people who are familiar with the status quo and current strategies that work. In addition, building a team of experts around you can provide you with the courage and confidence to accomplish what you may not consider possible on your own.

3. Create multiple sources of income over the course of years. Successful people generally have more than one or two streams of income, making them resilient against times when, due to some undesirable turn of events, they end up losing one source. You can always add new revenue-generating sources to your portfolio, a technique which one of my mentors aptly referred to

as animating your portfolio.

4. Don't quit. On many occasions, I found myself stuck, whether I had encountered issues with mortgages, available capital, or unpredictable business cycles, but I never quit. Instead, I focused on my goal, the things I had learned, and the knowledge from experts who surrounded me. Quitting when one is merely tired of facing barriers is not a good idea.

If I were to summarize the past decade of my life into one word of wisdom, that word would be courage. Be courageous when it comes to breaking into areas that terrify you. Break out of your comfort zone, because only then, with a clear goal, the right mentorship, and the courage to face the unknown, will you eventually find a way to achieve your goals and dreams.

Do Not Ask How.
Ask Why.

Author's Bio

Dr. Kevin Engel is an optometrist and owner of

a private practice in Lacombe, Alberta, Canada since 1999. On top of that, he's been an active real estate investor since 2010, who owns 78 properties in Central Alberta. He has received accolades, such as Creative Real Estate Investor of the Year in 2018 from the Real Estate Investment Network.

Dr. Engel is also a private lender who helps families and real estate investors with short-term capital to help them move forward. One of his other specialties is that he's an e-commerce entrepreneur, helping businesses and real estate investors animate their business and create new streams of revenue.

Websites:

🌐 lacombefamilyeyecare.ca

🌐 familyrealestate.ca

Contact info:

✉ drkevinjengel@gmail.com

📞 403-506-9839

Build Your
Personal Brand
for Times of Crisis

Mehrad Firouzi

Build Your Personal Brand for Times of Crisis

Mehrad Firouzi

The Premise

I believe that all men face crisis throughout their lives, so crisis is not a phenomenon requiring deep explanation. However, the effects of these challenges on our lives and businesses must be explored because each crisis can leave a different impact. Throughout such critical times, pain shall be bourne and lessons learned.

In what follows, I will attempt to depict a critical moment in my life. I am already certain that my attempt will fall short of illustrating the real experience as I felt it, but I do believe the lessons I took away can be shared with and used by many young managers and business owners.

Walking on the Edge of Failure

Years ago, I believed I had failed miserably in my life. I worried that I was good for nothing, for I had found nothing at which I excelled. I constantly looked for opportunities to learn and better myself, and my aspirations verged on obsession. Feeling frustrated and sad, I desperately hoped to make something of my life. I struggled through this strange period, trying everything I could think of to find a solution.

At the time, my father owned a big company, and if I worked

there, I could have a job many would wish for. Yet I did not want to be dependent on my father. I wanted to be able to stand on my own two feet. Nonetheless, after weighing my options, I thought my dad's company could give me a chance to go places. Therefore, I swallowed my pride and elected to work there.

Marketing and sales interested me greatly, so I read vigorously about them. I also read books and articles about personal development, because I wanted to utilize coaching skills to make changes in my life and in the lives of those around me.

Even though my father realized I was highly motivated, he thought I was too young to improve significantly in some areas and did not believe in my potential to make a difference at his company. Naturally, his critical view of my abilities negatively influenced the way his employees looked at me as well.

This experience proved so disheartening to me I decided against working for my dad before I truly even started. I had certainly never imagined my life to take such a challenging turn. The struggle between my obsession for success and my fear of taking risks left me feeling stranded.

To make matters even worse, I got into a fight with my father, and a second big crisis loomed on the horizon. However, I resolved to turn this crisis into fuel for success. At such a moment, others might have folded and told themselves, "There's no hope; it's over. I can no longer succeed," but this incident actually ignited my inner fire for chasing success. I needed to look for a way to turn this situation around. My father's words of distrust did not cause me to grow callous. On the contrary, they gave me tremendous motivation to work toward building my dream life.

After leaving the company and experiencing many ups and downs, I realized that everyone's trust in me would eventually come from my powerful personal brand. This golden key, which I did not formerly possess and felt the need to create as soon as possible, would enhance not only my business endeavors but also my whole life. A personal brand could be the solution to all my professional problems.

Crafting the Key

I attended tons of seminars, conferences, and lectures. During one of those lectures, a familiar speaker opened my eyes to the importance of building my own brand. At that seminar I met my dear mentor and trainer, Dr. Shahab Anari, to whom I owe a lot.

Only a few minutes spent beholding his presentation rekindled my inner fire. Dr. Anari's words inspired me to develop my personal brand and to pave a path that would lead toward the golden key. I promptly focused my efforts on cultivating a personal brand based on coaching.

Shortly thereafter, I found myself speaking, training, and coaching for insurance companies, service businesses, and manufacturing plants. My name gradually became widely known. After a certain point, even my father grew to be a fan of my work! He believed in me as a coach and as an individual capable of making significant changes. I achieved bliss, which I still enjoy to this day, and I will share some of my experiences with you.

After developing my Golden Key to Success methodology, I

managed to produce amazing results for my father's company. I was subsequently offered countless wonderful opportunities, including writing a book with Brian Tracy that I am very proud of.

The Golden Key Method

The key, which I will now expound upon, proves particularly useful for young managers; however, anyone can take advantage of it. The golden key system consists of the following four elements:

- Show people your brand in online environments
- Get to know your staff on deep levels
- Create competitive groups
- Set up mastermind meetings

Show people your brand in online environments

As a young manager, the first step I took involved reflecting on my abilities, values, life story, life mission, and personality. I put many thoughts on paper to identify my most unique characteristics. Then I shared these traits with my audience on the Internet, and people gradually came to recognize me as an expert in my field. I can emphatically say that mastering and utilizing the online world can shorten a ten-year path to a two-year one. As soon as people recognize and acknowledge you, your network will expand to a large extent in much less time. Online engagement will undoubtedly accelerate your progress as a young manager.

Get to know your staff on deep levels

I learned quickly that it becomes very costly for a company to train employees to act in a particular desired way. To combat this, when I first started consulting for my father's company, I scheduled meetings with each employee to get to know them better. The increased familiarity and comfort level helped tremendously in their opening up to me. Although I grew to be on friendly terms with the employees, I always acted professionally.

Once I knew the behavioral patterns of the employees, it became much easier to interact with them. This enabled their working at an optimal level of ability during a meeting or when I assigned a specific task to them. Cultivating strong relationships with my staff differentiated me from other young executives. My personal brand became inscribed in my employees' hearts as I genuinely earned their trust.

In times of crisis in business, a young manager may likely consider downsizing, which makes a lot of sense. However, before resorting to downsizing, I believe in applying methods to increase employee productivity. This can be accomplished through identifying behavioral strengths unique to each staff member and treating the individual workers accordingly. As a manager, positively influencing the behavior of the team and interacting often with the employees will earn you a more charismatic reputation and place your personal brand deep within their hearts. For example, I often start meetings by stating favorable qualities about employees, which makes them not only feel better but also want to listen carefully.

Thus, whenever facing crises, I maintain a primary strategy in which I help my employees modify their behavior, and if they do not change, I may let them go. Effective listening has helped me tremendously in getting to know my staff, and the questions I ask drive them to learn a lot. By clearly communicating the results I want to see and leaving it to them to decide how to go about achieving those goals, the pace of progress increases during times of crisis.

I constantly try to inscribe my personal brand in the hearts of workers by giving value to the team. In fact, a good understanding of the personalities of employees can help companies survive any crisis.

Create competitive groups

As John C. Maxwell said, "A [true] leader is one who knows the way, goes the way, and shows the way." I believe that struggling companies never simply have bad employees. Perhaps a leader does not know the way, or flaws exist in certain planning processes, but I consider nothing to be wrong with the employees in these situations. Reader, as a manager, your job is to assume the role of a real leader if you see that things are not running optimally.

I recall one meeting in particular when we noticed that some employees provided us with inaccurate information. We divided the staff into two groups to create competition between them and asked each group to share detailed daily reports. When Group A performed better than Group B, we encouraged Group A by giving positive feedback and asked Group B what they thought had contributed to the superior performance of Group A. This exercise dramatically increased people's learning pace and gave them the confidence to solve problems. In addition, the employees gradually became more committed to their work as a result of the friendly competition. Interestingly, the stronger the feedback I gave them, the happier my workers became, because they could recognize mistakes and try to correct or avoid making them in the future. Creating competitive groups holds true power in a business setting.

Remember that times of crisis are not moments best suited for giving negative feedback. As the commander of your army, to borrow a war analogy, you must lead staff members through the turmoil of the battle for success. If you remain dedicated to your job, your employees will be trained and willing to aim for the results you prefer. Simply ask them to do what you want to happen.

Set up mastermind meetings

On a weekly basis, I held sessions called Mastermind Meetings in the companies with which I engaged. During these, I expressed appreciation for the efforts of groups and employees who succeeded in gaining good results for the company. To encourage these highlighted individuals further, I introduced them in my personal social media accounts, and I also asked them to explain to others in the meeting how they managed to achieve such outstanding results. Not only did this help to strengthen my personal brand on social media platforms, it also increased the motivation of those working alongside me.

If we underwent a challenge in the company, we would often utilize mastermind meetings as a platform to search for a solution. In times of crisis, we increased the frequency of mastermind meetings online, and I acted like a commander of sorts. I did not give orders; instead, at short intervals, I set goals to get things done and formulated lists of tasks detailing the results I wanted. Throughout trying times, I continued providing ample encouragement and feedback. I advise you to allow your employees to do most of the talking and to respect their opinions. Your job is to ask the correct, important, and powerful questions, because being a listener works wonders.

Build Your Personal Brand for Times of Crisis

Author's Bio

I am **Mehrad Firouzi,** and I help young managers achieve four times their current performance in their business within six months. Over the last five years, I have helped multiple business owners cut their ten-year path into a two-year one. With over 1000 hours of experience in coaching small businesses and young entrepreneurs, I am ready to help you on your six-month journey. To get to know me better, you can find me on LinkedIn, Instagram, Facebook, and Twitter under mehrad.firouzi, or you can visit my website at www.mehradfirouzi.com.

Believe and
You Will Achieve

Dr. Leila Hojabri

Believe and You Will Achieve
Dr. Leila Hojabri

How many of you decided to start your business in Canada, found it difficult and gave up on the idea before you reached success? If your answer to the question is affirmative, do not panic. You are not alone! Especially if you are an immigrant, you will encounter many challenges while launching your business idea.

By learning from other people's and my own experience, as well as reading many books, I learned that you can switch from being an employee to be a business owner if you are able to change your programmed mindset. Having a clear business idea, adequate research about that industry, and deep knowledge of yourself and what motivates you will help you stay on track to success. Keeping an open mind and a sharp focus on your desire will bring about the opportunities you seek in their best timing. Then, in that ideal moment, it is up to you to open your opportune gift and start executing your dream, or you may just lose it due to inaction!

Some people are brave enough to give up full-time employment to start a business from scratch; others prefer a more secure transition. The journey of my life illustrates various attempts to start a business and what outcomes eventually happened. I always consider myself a student who learns from failures, and I hope to convey my findings to you in this chapter.

I was considered a successful student throughout my academic years, studying twenty-four years in three schools, four universities, and a college. I studied for two reasons: first, I was in love with learning, and second, education was the bridge to a more attractive and broader future. Higher education could connect me to other passionate and determined professionals. This pathway was the safest and surest way to brilliant social and financial opportunities in the parameters of my home country, Iran. Immersed in academia, I was in pure harmony with my world. At the same time, in order to quench my curiosity, I sought opportunities to explore cultures and societies beyond the borders of Iran.

My Planned Future Didn't Quite Happen

After immigration to Canada, my desired professional life was to be a faculty member, just as I had planned during my Ph.D. and post-doctoral years of training. That expected future did not happen for me, so I revisited my professional goals and dreams.

I was a research associate in Trent University, when I got pregnant for the second time. Unfortunately, I lost my job after maternity leave. Therefore, I accepted two other contract jobs in Trent University which were seasonal and temporary. At this point, an old dream of mine rekindled: starting my own business!

I started exploring ideas I had for businesses in various fields, most of which related to sustainably serving the environment. These ideas ranged from manufacturing valuable products from restaurant and fast-food waste oils, to preparing "green" cosmetics from renewable sources, and lots of other environmentally friendly ideas. As a new immigrant living in the small city of Peterborough, Ontario, and with a limited budget, I believed executing these ideas was beyond my ability. I decided to give up on those and focus on finding employment until I was better prepared to pursue my dreams. I pressed a pause button on my goal, yet I was sure I would not forget it.

Entrepreneurial Seed in Me

The first time I thought about entrepreneurship was as a Bachelor of Science student in Chemistry. I had just returned from a scientific field trip to a factory that specialized in extracting essential oils from medicinal plants. During a friendly dream-building conversation with my friends, I discovered for the first time how exciting the world of entrepreneurship could be. It became a very clearly visualized dream that I would have my own business in the future. Later, after studying and researching for another seven years, I absolutely had forgotten about that entrepreneurial vision, until I lost my job and became frustrated with holding temporary jobs and the uncertainties that went along with that status. I wonder if this situation sounds familiar to you, especially if you are a newcomer.

Though I was not prepared to start my own business yet, I decided to enter the world of industry, because my family had relocated to the bigger city of Ottawa. Since I didn't have any industry experience, finding the right job was a challenge.

I finally decided to accept an offer from World-Skills, one of the most amazing places for helping immigrant professionals, and I applied for the Advanced Biotechnology program for immigrants in Algonquin College. The most appealing part of this program was that it offered a CO-OP opportunity, which would lead to a permanent job in the industry. This was exactly what I hoped for at the time.

A Turning Point

After a few years, due to some policy changes at the company, some of my coworkers, including my supervisor, lost their jobs, and for the third time, I received a sign from the universe how important it was to be my own boss. On the one hand, I felt anxious and insecure in my career, and on the other hand, as a mother and a spouse with financial responsibility, I was not quite ready to shift to the business owner's world. I found it wiser to build a side business and expand it over time.

I explored and took action on some of my ideas, including:

- Preparing handmade candles with cultural artwork printed on them
- Exploring online selling in Etsy, Shopify, E-bay, and Amazon
- Importing cultural products from Iran to Canada

Several reasons prevented those ideas from expanding into viable businesses; for instance, me not resonating with online sales and working with a niche market that was too small to be lucrative.

Those Who Seek Will Find

While I explored my various options, I took part in a seminar by World Financial Group (WFG). WFG is a brokerage company and partner with some banks and financial institutions, and it is a platform that can help you become self-employed and business owner. Consulting with my spouse, I decided to pursue and learn financial knowledge and learn more about other business opportunities at the same time.

I was not currently able to see the full potential of the business, especially because there were some negative rumors circulating about WFG. This prompted me to postpone building my business at least two months. As I learned more about the financial industry, I observed my office's work culture, experienced its mentoring support, and connected with many successful business owners in the company. All of this completely changed my wary mindset about WFG.

There it was; I now had all the pieces to my puzzle. In the past, I had even considered purchasing a franchise, but I was not able to risk the money. Here I could build a franchise with support from peers and leaders in the WFG company, and I could do so with no money down! What I needed was the ability to build a great team. Leadership and teamwork skills are crucial to entrepreneurial success.

All my doubts disappeared as I researched the business model for my new company. Clarity about the business model and seeing the potential client pool within my family and circle of friends inspired me to promptly complete the government licensing component and speed up the business establishment process.

The Transition Was Hard

Starting my own business revealed my strengths and weaknesses. Acknowledging my strengths acted as an energy battery for me to work on my weaknesses. I looked for solutions to overcome any fears. Coming from a very technical background with limited customer service experience, I had to challenge myself to communicate and network effectively. These factors are very crucial for any business owner that wants to grow. In my previous experiences, students, coworkers, and supervisors approached me for instruction and help. In this new situation, I was the one reaching out to others to assist with my business matters.

I dug deep within and discovered something inhibiting me, my fear of rejection! I was absolutely sure if I could overcome this challenge, I would experience great growth in my business. To overcome my fear, I must become stronger mentally. I regularly grew uncomfortable with competitors' criticism, another area needing improvement. Attending some self-development courses really assisted me to address these weaknesses.

I started a self-growth journey to become a more qualified and stronger person, regardless of any external factors. I learned if I wanted to be successful in business, something inside me had to change: my perception of the world. I learned from Mary Manin Morrissey that in any situation, I could play victim or victor. The choice is always mine. My eagerness to teach and my presentation skills were strengths I could use to my clients' and my own benefit. These traits helped me become a better communicator.

The Lessons I Learned

Switching from employment to business owner is not the right choice for everybody. Some people like to be physically and mentally involved with job duties only during work hours. They prefer to follow a clear job description and enjoy the security of a salary at the end of the month. In contrast, there are people who look for more challenges and opportunities than holding a regular job will provide. They prefer to have freedom of choice in how to spend their time. They are ambitious, self-motivated, and have creative initiative. This group will likely find entrepreneurship more suitable, and they could benefit from my story.

If you currently hold a regular job that doesn't satisfy you, and you think you are entrepreneurial, you may find your situation frustrating. You know you are not able to dramatically change the condition of your present employment, and a raise in salary cannot adequately meet your true desires. Right now, your job description may seem repetitive and boring. You are subject to losing your job any time your company cannot afford your salary or does not require your skillset anymore. These reasons, and many more, reveal why it is optimal for you to take action toward building your dream.

If you decide to choose entrepreneurship, these few key points may accelerate your journey:

1. The first step is to clarify what type of business suits your goals and personality. You may consult with a career coach to find out which pathway motivates you the most and takes you to a higher and more satisfying energy level. Your effort at this stage will pay off by accelerating your success later.

2. When you are clear on your choice, look for possible steps to achieve your goal. You may need to learn technical knowledge. You may want to work on your self-development.

Maybe working on your soft skills is the key element. All of these skills will help you stand out in your industry while making you more credible.

3. Consider finding a great mentor in the area of your business or finding a system that is already set up to ease the transition. I succeeded in the financial industry because I was able to connect with mentors and followed a proven system.

4. Step out of your comfort zone. Going to networking events, practicing public speaking, facing your fears, and changing your daily routines are some examples of broadening your comfort zone. Remember, great opportunities can be found outside of your comfort zone, and they are waiting for you to take action!

5. After a period of hard work, pause, experience quality time, and relax. Consider meditation and other techniques to ease any stress you may feel. This periodic practice will give you the opportunity to think deeply and find more opportunities. Taking time to relax is a great opportunity to clear your mind of unnecessary and negative thoughts and to create the clarity that can open a lot of doors for you.

The transition from employee to entrepreneur, no matter how difficult it may seem, is possible if you have the right mindset. Be prepared to lose a bit of comfort and face new challenges in order to achieve success. Starting a business gives you a great opportunity for personal advancement that you will likely never achieve in a regular job. Treading on this path is like going to school to learn how to live a new life. There are always new things to learn; and that's the beauty of the process, if you're a growth-minded person.

Whether you decide to make the transition gradually or in one step, deep self-knowledge and building on strengths while improving weaknesses will help you establish a successful business. I hope this chapter is a much-needed nudge for you to take your first steps and pursue your dreams!

Believe and You Will Achieve

Author's Bio

Dr. Leila Hojabri is an energetic supportive entrepreneur within the financial services industry. She helps individuals, business owners, and families reach their goals and dreams by educating and empowering them with financial literacy, and by offering them the best financial solutions and services.

Also, she shares her professional experiences with motivated and ambitious individuals who would like to start their entrepreneurship journey with her team, and she supports them in all stages of the transition. She has experienced eight different academic and industrial environments which include working in, researching, supervising, and managing people in three countries before starting venturing into finance.

Apart from co-authoring "Bounce back to Success" with Brian Tracy, she has published twenty scientific papers in international journals. She spends her spare time reading books and attending quality workshops and programs to increase her knowledge and skills. Her vision for herself, her family, and her team is to rise up mentally and live a vision-driven life, instead of being in a reactive mode.

You can find her at:

- ✉ leila.hojabri@gmail.com
- 🌐 agents.wfgcanada.ca/on/north-york/leila-hojabri
- 📷 www.instagram.com/leilahojabr/
- f www.facebook.com/leila.hojabri
- in www.linkedin.com/in/leila-hojabri-6a881038/

The Pregnancy Test
That Made the Difference

Nasrin Husseini

The Pregnancy Test That Made the Difference
Nasrin Husseini

Cultural Breakthrough

The turning point stands crystal clear in my mind. I was a student in the Veterinary School at Kabul University in 2010. Our internal medicine professor asked each student to do a pregnancy test on a dairy cow. All the boys in our class did the vaginal exam without a problem, and then they stared at the only two women in the class, watching to see what we would do.

In those days in Afghanistan, veterinary medicine was not considered a suitable profession for women in our society. We were the only two women in a class of eighty-nine male students. My friend did not perform the test. All eyes were now on me! I had to make a decision: either to follow what others expect me to do or do what I think is right. I could back off and not perform the test and live the life others wanted me to live, or I could perform the test, be the topic of ridicule for a few days but bring about the change and make it ordinary for other women to perform this test!

That day, when my friend did not perform the pregnancy test, she sealed her decision that the field of veterinary medicine was not "right" for her as a woman. But I was not deterred. I told my professor and classmates, "This is the field I chose, and I will perform all the required tests." I was certainly nervous and shaking, but I pulled myself together and decided, "No matter what, I will perform the test."

While I performed the vaginal exam, with my arm disappearing all the way up to my elbow, one of the boys in our class took a photo to show others in mockery of me. However, I was proud I was fulfilling all the requirements of the program. I even wished for a copy of that photo to post in my room as a souvenir of my success.

Experiencing Empowerment

I felt empowered even though they all were laughing. Nonetheless, all the laughs and jeers affected my self-esteem. There are many times like this in our lives when we care more about what people think than about what makes us truly happy. The bitterness of that moment disappeared after a while, but the sweetness of my success will stay with me forever.

In another similar scenario, our class attended a field trip to a farm to learn and watch artificial insemination in cows. Again, my female classmate stayed away and did not watch, because she thought it was not appropriate for a woman to watch such a thing in front of those many boys. Nonetheless, that was veterinary medicine and part of our curriculum. Because I was shorter in height than the guys, I went to the front of the line and closely observed the artificial insemination.

I decided to be in veterinary medicine, and I am either all in or all out; and that decision required me to be resilient, brave and willing to be the topic of gossip. As in other medical programs, we performed all these tests in fifth year of university, and by that time there were a few other women entering the program. I wanted them to feel brave and perform these tests when it was their turn. I wanted this to be the new normal for everyone in our academic discipline.

Numerous professors in the university tried to encourage me to leave the veterinary program and pursue something more suitable for women. This was hard to understand since these were the most educated people in our country. This was very discouraging; however, there are times when the right people say the wrong things. I had tremendous support from my family, my father, and my grandpa. Therefore, in spite of all the discouraging experiences, I kept moving forward.

A Dream Comes True

Living in a country where, as a woman, you are not to be seen, heard or trusted to make a decision is extremely demoralizing. Dreams of a life with a better future in another country are extremely attractive. Having graduated as the top student of my veterinary class in 2010, I was able to receive a leadership scholarship and travel to the United States. From there, my dream came true! I made my way to Canada and applied for refugee status. Canada opened new doors of opportunity for me. Finally, I was somewhere that my body and spirit could both be at peace, and I could call it home!

In Canada, I began the journey to develop the best version of myself that I possibly could. I had to work extra hard to find myself in this new country. I began to recognize and examine the depth of my emotional scars so that I could heal them.

Once I entered the free world, I came to feel how lost I had been and to understand how hurtful my prior experiences were. However, the good news is that it is never too late to find healing for yourself and have the opportunity to help others as a result. I started reading novels and self-help books and felt calmed by the books in a very unexpected way. I was not used to reading outside of the curriculum in Afghanistan. Reading allowed me to recognize and understand that it was no wonder I experienced all those discriminations and emotional discomforts there. Years of trauma, being a refugee, and experiencing all those difficulties had left deep emotional scars.

Lost in a New Country

Having little experience in making decisions for myself, I initially felt very lost and confused about making wise choices. For years, I had been told what to do and what was the best for me to do. Even though I was raised in an open-minded family with five sisters and no brothers, I still felt my inadequacies as a woman. My parents were ridiculed for not having any sons, but they loved us and wanted us to succeed.

Outside of our home, it was another matter. As a woman, I was never right, no one would listen, and men were always right no matter how wrong they were! This was just an engrained fact of life for Afghan women.

Becoming Resilient and Strong

In Canada, I felt homesick. I missed my parents, my sisters, and my friends, but I was determined to succeed and to continue my education. Barriers stood in the way, as it took four years to receive my permanent residency status. This meant, during that time, I was stateless, and I was not eligible for a government student loan. Those who are in this situation understand very well what I endured. I think the most important thing I did was to keep myself mentally healthy and not let myself go insane. I read novels so that for a while I could escape from my own life and be in a different imaginary world. That always gave me peace and happiness.

I worked and kept myself busy, so I didn't have the time to think about my current situation and stress about it. Whenever I was feeling down or disappointed, I went for a long walk or to a theater to watch a movie. I would tell myself that better days will come. Things were not in my control; the only thing I could do was wait and pray. I prayed a lot and that was so comforting for me. I was happy God was there for me always, no matter what the situation. I could have picked an easier path and simply married one of the many people who proposed to me in Canada, receive my landed immigrant status, and have a normal life. But I had a bigger goal, and I decided to stick with the rougher path, the one that would lead to a beautiful place.

I worked as a tutor or after-school teacher in order to put food on my table. I dreamed of the day I might pursue more education in Canada. I believed education was important to my future success and acceptance. Nothing would stop me, as I took one baby step at a time. I was always searching for the best solution to each circumstance or situation I faced. Tutoring, volunteering, and being in the community helped me take care of my mental health.

Seeking relief from my loneliness and the uncertainty I faced in this country, I sought comfort from the Afghan community within Canada. Sadly, some in the community did not approve of a woman who travelled alone. They would gossip and look at me differently, only because I was also living alone. And because I was alone, men thought it was a green light for them to approach me. Turning them away, at times, I had to face them angrily. They made me feel I was the guilty one and only because I was living alone. I refused to let negative people alter the good goals I had for my life.

Finding My Way

Education and learning had always contributed to my peace. As I continued searching down that path, I found an organization that evaluated my Afghan documents and converted my grades into the Canadian system. I had to work two jobs in order to support myself and pay for my educational expenses, but in Canada this was possible.

I didn't qualify for any of the government assistance programs, so I had to work very hard in order to further my immigration status faster. Nonetheless, I loved to work. I'd learned that hard work never hurt anyone, and I was happy to be kept busy. Arriving home very late each evening, I had very little time to feel homesick. So, being tired, I'd just go straight to bed.

I'd always wanted to complete a Master of Science degree in animal health and then possibly consider a PhD. However, in order to enroll in such a university program, I'd have to pay international student tuition and fees, since I did not yet have Canadian status. This was impossible for me to afford. Therefore, I enrolled in an online Master of Education. This was more affordable and would give me a degree which would help me in the future.

My dream was always to work in veterinary medicine, and I had graduated at the top in my veterinary class in Afghanistan. Other female students and faculty back in Afghanistan were watching me. I was always seen as their role model. They were watching me through social media, so I did not want to send a wrong message. There are times in life that we do not live solely for ourselves but also for others. This is especially true if we have responsibilities as a role model. I wanted to show other Afghan women that it is possible to succeed.

Waiting four years to gain Canadian immigration status, it took longer to get where I am today than I initially anticipated, because I had to work and study at the same time. I eventually registered my documents with the Canadian Veterinary Medical Association (CVMA) in order to take my licensing exam and practice veterinary medicine in Canada. It was around that time in 2015, I received my permanent Canadian residency status. The first thing I did was to contact the University of Guelph where the oldest veterinary college in North America is located, the Ontario Veterinary College (OVC).

The Opening of Educational Doors

Wonderfully, at the University of Guelph I met my college program advisor, whom to this day I call my angel. She was the first person who listened carefully to me and heard my life story. She was so kind to me, like a mom, as she could see all my scars. How satisfying it was to have someone with whom I could share all my pain and sense that she could feel and understand it. I started my master's program at OVC with her guidance, and then I applied for a university scholarship.

My dreams were starting to come true. Out of two hundred applicants from around the world, I was selected to be one of the first to receive the prestigious Arrell Graduate Scholarship from the University of Guelph. That scholarship changed my life. I could then afford my living expenses, paying for my studies, and I could help my family while I studied. It is very hard to study when you're not financially stable.

I could have asked my dad for money, but there were my five sisters to raise. I did not want to be a burden to my family; I was the one who was supposed to help them. The pieces of the puzzle of my life started to fall into place, and I started to feel better. I could feel I was healing from the inside out. My mind was clearer now, and it was easier to make my own decisions. Good days were on the horizon!

Serving as a Role Model for Women

There were many families back home watching me. I was the first woman in our area and among our relatives who traveled alone and was living alone. If I could succeed, this would open many doors for the other women in our family and in our area. People would let their daughters study and travel, if they saw it was possible to succeed and thrive in a new land. I felt I was in a very strategic position.

Now, as I graduate with a Master of Science degree, people in our area and our relatives use my example as a role model for their daughters. They're letting their daughters study and even travel, trusting they can also make the tough journey to a bright future with new hopes and dreams.

Living four years without permanent residence status, feeling like a drifter, I had the most difficult time of my life. However, eventually, I realized this was something out of my control. I had to simply be patient, persistent, and press on. The good thing about difficult days is that nothing will look difficult to you after you pass through them successfully. The moment you fall down, you do not think, "Shall I get up or not?" You automatically stand up and continue your journey. When you face a problem, you don't get stuck on the problem, you automatically focus on finding a solution. You realize the harder you fall down, the stronger you will rise. I fell down many times in my journey, and I went through many hard situations. However, all those tough times have shaped who I am today! I am truly thankful for my very difficult journey, for it has resulted in the wonderful life I enjoy today.

The Pregnancy Test That Made the Difference

Author's Bio

I am originally from Afghanistan. I was raised and grew up with my other 5 sisters in an average family in the province of Bamyan. Due to the ongoing war, when I was a child, we sought refugee status in Iran, and it was in Iran that I finished my high school with honors graduating top of my class. After the Taliban period, in 2004, my dad decided we should go back to Afghanistan so that we could go to university and continue our education there. I got into Veterinary School in Afghanistan when it was a huge deal for a girl to be a vet.

The more the society tried to push me down, the harder I tried to stand up and it was then that I was able to prove a girl can also be a veterinarian if she is given the proper opportunity. Almost every semester, I was at the top of my class, a class full of male peers. However, the society kept denying my abilities. I managed to win the respect of my professors and peers as I became the first woman to graduate on top from that DVM program after Taliban period. I eventually graduated top of my class in 2011. Subsequently, I was offered a Women's Leadership Scholarship by Green River College in Washington State, USA and then I made my way to Canada.

Since arriving in Canada in 2010, I have worked at the Toronto Humane Society, the Donland Animal Hospital, and the Kato Animal Hospital in Toronto. These jobs have helped me familiarize myself with veterinary practice in Canada.

I completed my MSc degree in Immunology at the University of Guelph and received Arrell Scholarship, which is a prestigious scholarship at the University of Guelph. Currently, I am working as a research assistant at the University of Guelph.

You can connect with me on LinkedIn and Instagram.

in www.linkedin.com/in/nasrin-husseini-072563161

○ nasveterinary

Don't Let Your Current Situation Stop You from Going After Your **Dreams**

Ramin Jafarizadeh

Don't Let Your Current Situation Stop You from Going After Your Dreams

Ramin Jafarizadeh

In an environment of service and competition, business has always been both a challenge and a reward. It could either make you rich or set you back in a number of ways you may find hard to believe. My story illustrates how I was able to win in business and, ultimately, learn how to win in life as well.

Oman, 2016

Three partners and I were engaged in the signboard workshop business. One of my partners was in dire financial straits. He was actually bankrupt at that time. Luckily, he received a substantial amount of money from a deal in which he was involved, and he was eventually able to join us. Time passed and business was moving forward. We marketed and were able to secure a few big projects from shopping malls and large hypermarkets.

Just to give you an idea of the size of our signboards, we averaged 40-50 sqm per piece. And the biggest one was 150x3 m, made during the first year we started the company. Things were looking good. It felt like we were on our way.

Seemingly Insurmountable Challenges

After a year of getting projects and doing collection activities, it became apparent our customers were not making their payments. And I gradually started facing a litany of problems.

In addition, I issued a guarantee check to one of my partners, so I could help him purchase a shop for his relatives. This was a bad decision, which would later contribute to my financial woes.

Within one short year, our signboard business was making a nosedive. I even had to use my own personal funds in an attempt to support the business. In fact, I ended up going bankrupt trying to save the business.

Budgeting difficulties and cash flow problems began to surface. We fell into debt; salaries were delayed; we couldn't pay the rent; and we had to deal with mounting bills from our suppliers.

For some reason, our customers were not paying us, and there was little to no revenue coming in. I eventually figured out that our customers had formerly worked with one of my partners who owed them money, and he hadn't even bothered to tell me about it.

To make matters worse, the guarantee check I had issued bounced. Things heated up, and for the first time in my life, a complaint was lodged against me.

Personal Situation

My problems did not end there. My wife began to complain about our financial problems. Within a month, she decided to go back to our home country, Iran, and within two months she was already asking for a divorce.

You might know that for a foreigner to operate in Oman, you have to have a local sponsor. To exacerbate my situation even further, my local sponsor decided to let me go, because he said I had tarnished his reputation in the government (due to the bounced cheque). As fate would have it, he was a member of a prestigious family in Oman.

Rock Bottom

So there I was, at the lowest place in my life. No cash in the bank. No credit from the bank. We had failed to pay our fifteen employees their salaries. We had pending projects that were not going forward. And we had too many receivables. I was receiving 200+ daily phone calls from creditors, my local sponsor, tenants and other parties.

Even my wife, who finally filed for divorce, demanded her alimony (500 golden coins, equivalent to 4 kgs of gold) from me. All In all, it took me nine months to settle these money problems with too many details to cover in this book. Basically, I lost everything: my wife, my savings, and even my local sponsor.

The Great Comeback

In May of 2018, it became clear to me that I had two options on the table:

1. I could file a case against my partner to recoup the money from the guarantee check, and at the same time start negotiating and collecting payments from my long-overdue customers. This sounded like a reasonable solution. I would be getting a lot of money, which could put me back on the scene and help me hit the ground running. An average person would think some retaliation wouldn't hurt either.

2. Forget my receivables and start again.

Considering each of the two scenarios, it was a very difficult decision to make. How can you forget the people who have put you through hell? Forgetting went against everything I knew and believed as a person and as a businessman. Should I forget my rights and let them loose? Forget about the money I worked so hard to earn? I wondered, "Wouldn't that mean I'm a coward? Wouldn't it mean I'm not the warrior I'm supposed to be, learning from challenges and making them right?"

How I Found My Way Back to Success

Making a Decision

Finally, after much thought and reflection, I pulled myself together and decided to go for the second option. I decided to forget what people owed me and start from scratch. It pained me when I realized this was not the first time I was doing this. It was actually the fourth time I was starting anew. I can't express in words how difficult it was each time. However, it was far more painful this time. If starting from scratch in my past endeavors felt like a bad headache, this time it felt like losing one of my hands. It was terrible. But just like any other major decision in life, I made it and stuck to it.

Focusing on the Future

I knew that if I chose to start from ground zero, I had to focus on the future and not ruminate about the past. I could hardly imagine how I would be able to erase all that happened from my memory, and simply think about the future. To me, it initially seemed almost impossible. But I had no other choice. I simply had to go on to the best of my ability.

Acting on My Decision, One Step at a Time

Making a decision means nothing if you do not act on it. I went all in and I gave it all I had. I woke up at 5 AM every day, and I did anything and everything necessary to get myself out of that situation.

Eventually, as I persevered and kept working on solving my problems, my situation began to ease. Things started to look a bit brighter. I decided to join a friend's company, which tremendously helped me get back on my feet. I was even recognized and honored for increasing his sales tenfold and doubling his sales team in a span of just one year.

This happened around the same time the company's competitors were languishing due to a new tax law that did little to boost business. Incidentally, we also won the award for the best corporation of that same year. Around that time, I decided to start a new business, a freight forwarding company.

Presently, I co-operate the freight business with some like-minded colleagues who are currently doing very well in sales. I'm now also venturing into the website marketplace to take advantage of a fast-growing market.

On the Way Up

It's been two years since my business was struck with a

whirlwind of troubles. Now that I look back, I am pretty convinced I made the right decision. I was certain then, and I'm more certain now, if I had followed what I call those "dead collections", I wouldn't have been able to accomplish the things I have within the last two years.

I could have wasted my time being in a legal environment negotiating with people who think they will become millionaires just by hoodwinking others and not paying their debts. It would be just another "Mind-Erosion Game". I'm glad I didn't even start down that road. It would have cost me precious time and my sanity.

The core message of this chapter is: Don't let your current situation stop you from going after your dream.

Sometimes you have to pivot. Sometimes you need to change, despite your initial intentions. Now I'd like to share with you some tips that helped me get unstuck and bounce back to success.

Review Your Past Successes

Although it makes perfect sense to evaluate what went wrong so you can learn from that, it is equally useful to take stock of the things you did right. A lot of times, when we recount the memories of what we have done correctly in the past, we see that we already know what to do. This process will ultimately save you time and prevent the heartbreak of failure.

Learn from Your Mistakes

You can never totally avoid making mistakes, and they eventually allow you to learn and grow your business. What is important is that you should be resilient enough to keep going, to persevere, especially when it seems nothing is working in your favor.

One Step at a Time

Be patient while working your way back to solid footing and take it one day at a time. Create S.M.A.R.T. goals, meaning goals that are Specific, Measurable, Achievable, Realistic and Time-Bound. This way, when setting goals, you know exactly the desired result, and the deadline to achieve it.

Don't Fool Yourself; Pay Attention to the Facts

Business downturns are a blessing in disguise because they help you set more realistic goals in the future. You acquire the knowledge of what works and what doesn't. Keep your eye on the ball.

Monitor the results and always pay attention. Especially if you're starting a new business, know the industry you're entering. Make sure you understand the fundamentals and the rules of success. Study the business model as well as the market. Mastery of both will guarantee you are profitable. It will also guarantee your longevity in the market and guard against committing mistakes and possible bankruptcy. If you know your business, inside and out, even if anything untoward happens, like a market downturn, you will have the ability to save yourself from losses and to adapt quickly. This enables you to go on and still profit when everybody else is suffering losses.

Change Your Thoughts and Actions

No business plan is ironclad. If your business plan isn't working, scrap it. Create another one. Your habits and beliefs need constant revision and changes. Learn to be flexible. The market is constantly changing. Always be ready to adapt, because in business, change is the only thing that's constant.

Lastly, evaluate your target market. Even if you have a great business idea, if there is no demand or market for it, your products won't sell. If you look hard enough, you can always find a specific product and match it with a relevant market. A product that is not specific may end up with no market, and that means no sales and no growth. Learn to target the people who have the need for your product, and sales will follow.

Conclusion

Overall, I can say that the most valuable asset a person has is time. Time can even be more valuable than other material resources. That's because time, like money, is subject to compound interest. Sometimes, it's better to stop pursuing a dead end, and instead, invest in a new activity that can multiply over time. This is exactly what I did when I made the decision not to go after the outstanding accounts. Instead, I made myself productive and started investing in the future by starting a new endeavor that paid off handsomely.

Don't let your current situation discourage you from reaching for your dreams.

*Don't Let
Your Current
Situation Stop
You from Going
After Your Dreams*

Author's Bio

Ramin Jafarizadeh is a self-made multilingual
entrepreneur. He started working at 13 just out of his unstoppable
interest in business (not because he needed money) and immigrated
to Oman on his own at the ripe age of 20.

He has tried his hand at various industries such as Media and
Marketing, Computer Science, Tourism, Shipping and Trading,
Manufacturing, Renewable Energies, Education, Distributions,
Advertisement and Signage, Retail, and more. Drawing on his
engineering background and combining it with his vast business
knowledge, he always tries to analyze any situation and make the
best entrepreneurial decision. He believes that one's habits and
environment can make all the difference. Ramin takes pride is

the fact that he has consistently tried his best to move forward by learning from his failures.

In the past few years, he has been involved in the startup ecosystem, and he has built efficient ways of doing business along the way. He was named "Best Personal Brand" by MENAA in Oct 2019 because of his network in different countries. Along with other big corporations and airlines, he also received the "Best Corporate Award" because he was able to 10+X his sales and grab a huge share of his market.

You can connect with Ramin on LinkedIn.

Quitting

Can Be a Good Thing

Amirreza Kamalian

Quitting Can Be a Good Thing
Amirreza Kamalian

An Uninvited Conflict

I could not change what had happened. Failure loomed on the horizon and rendered me helpless. A business rival of mine, considered among the best in the animal feed market, decided to push me out of the market by playing the price game. I saw my business fall apart right in front of me as I learned I could not sell any of my recently imported cargo, even at break-even prices. I could do naught but watch my efforts fade away into the abyss.

At only twenty-five years of age, I started a lucrative importing business in Iran. Although I had studied civil engineering and my family had established a construction business in which I could have easily become involved, I conducted some research to see if I could find a better source of income. Eventually, I decided to begin importing animal feed from China to distribute among wholesalers in Iran. In the beginning, I dealt with small amounts, but after four years, my imported cargos increased about thirty times in size. I considered my business rather successful, and under the right circumstances, I earned significant profits with each shipment.

I quickly made a name for myself as an important player in the business, but little did I know that all the attention I received would not necessarily lead to better sales and higher profits. Before my showing up on the scene, one Mr. M. had effectively monopolized the entire animal feed importing market. He could name any price for his goods, and everybody would have to buy from him because no other supplier alternatives existed. Once I posed a threat to Mr. M., he resorted to removing me from the scene to maintain his hold on the market.

I had just imported a huge cargo from China when I learned Mr. M. sliced his prices in half. I stood to lose a lot of money. I could not return the merchandise, because once the ships departed from China, there was no going back; I had signed an irrevocable contract with my Chinese suppliers. Despite the big loss suffered from that shipment, I elected to keep moving forward since I previously made quite a lot of money and believed I could survive if I held on. Slashed prices did not present the only challenge to my business, however. Suddenly, all kinds of problems began popping up. On one instance, my merchandise was held up in the Customs Department for forty-five days, with agents from the Ministry of Health snooping around. The agents gathered samples for extra testing at their laboratories, a procedure taking even more time. In my time as an importer, I had never encountered investigations of this nature before. Only much later did I connect the dots and realize that rather than coincidences, these mysterious delays belonged to the same scheme designed by Mr. M.

While my shipment remained stuck in Customs, selling prices continued dropping. After unsuccessfully trying to wait out the declining prices, I finally managed to sell my product – at a huge loss. Knowing that ups and downs characterize any sort of business, I felt determined to prove that I would endure in this market although my business had taken a nosedive. I did not want

QUITTING CAN BE A GOOD THING

to accept that someone had outplayed me. Unfortunately, some merchandise in my next shipment expired because customers now refused to buy from me, and I did not own the types of facilities necessary for long-term warehousing.

When I investigated further to find out the real cause of my problems, I discovered with the help of a former customer the name of the man behind the scenes. I remembered Mr. M. as one of the major players in the market, but I could not believe he would cause me so much trouble. I found myself in a losing battle with him, and my losses kept piling up.

A New Dawn

Around the same time, my father applied for immigration to Canada, and I had the opportunity to join him. I liked Iran and felt satisfied with my life there but, given my desperation in finding the way out of my troubles, I took my chances and moved to Canada where I could hope for a fresh start.

I expected improved chances for success in Canada. Unlike in Iran, pig farming represented a major Canadian business, increasing my target market even more. Connections I had already established in China would also give me a head start. However, I soon realized that working in Canada came with its own set of challenges. Chinese goods did not carry a good reputation in the Canadian market. Furthermore, like back home, the Canadian market contained several major competitors. While I received much better treatment in Canada, I faced the challenge of creating my business network from scratch. Thankfully, I found ways to expedite and simplify this transition. I attended farming expos to familiarize myself with the unique market and to establish reliable customers. I even tried my hand at franchising for a while. Customers in Canada often refused to deal with me because they had established long-standing relationships with trustworthy suppliers who succeeded in this business for generations. The language barrier posed another significant problem for me, especially when dealing with farmers, many of whom used non-standard English.

In the end, I found my knowledge of this new market to be inadequate. Even when I did manage to make a sale, insignificant profits caused the minimal reward to appear not worth the effort. At this juncture, I chose to call it quits.

Since I wanted to try something entirely new, I considered two serious options for my next career move: office rentals and land development. Through extensive research, I discovered a few key ingredients of a successful office rental business. First, success required the proper location, ideally a high-rise building in the heart of a big city. I soon realized the market had already filled such locations. Second, renting office spaces required a huge financial investment upfront. This posed a great risk for me, because a lot of big players already maintained quite solid positions in the market. Third, I somehow needed to acquire the right customers, such as big firms with many employees that could rent entire floors of a building. I worried that finding such customers and convincing them to trust me would not be possible in my situation.

In the end, I decided against opening an office rental business until a time when I felt prepared for such a huge undertaking. To this day, I think I might give it a shot in the future.

Since I studied civil engineering at university and some family members worked in the field, I switched to the construction field. I opted to try my hand at a more specialized type of construction work, namely, land severance and development. However, to succeed in working under this specialization required gaining a specific understanding of the market, so I decided to work at a development company first.

Having functioned as an entrepreneur from an early age, I found working for somebody else quite difficult. I believed that working on my own and using my time as I saw fit proved much more profitable than sticking to a traditional 9-to-5 schedule. Nevertheless, I followed through with my plan to start as an employee, recognizing that I must familiarize myself with the market. Land severance and development also required hefty investments, so I wanted to proceed as carefully as possible, one step at a time, and leave little room for mistakes.

I stayed at the development company for quite a while, learning how to handle different types of projects and giving myself a chance to learn the ropes, so I could later build my own business on a solid foundation. This process took over a year and a half, longer than I initially anticipated, but in the end, I considered the commitment worth it. I gained enough experience and expertise to confidently start my own business. In 2016, I successfully completed my first land development project, which resulted in a sizeable profit.

Throughout this time, I often thought about going back to Iran, but I concluded that if I made this choice, I would be giving up on a great opportunity for success in Canada. I felt confident I could make my land development business prosper. Fortunately, this career path worked out well for me in the end, and I no longer doubt my decision to stay in Canada.

In Hindsight

The challenge I faced in Iran, while a difficult experience, taught me some important lessons. First, each industry comes with its own set of rules which must be followed by anyone who wishes to succeed. No matter who you are, how determined you are, or how hard you work, if you do not play according to the rules, you will be knocked out. Second, people who hold positions of power in each business tend to set the rules. Unless you are one of these individuals, you must comply with their rules a lot of the time if you want to find success. Ignoring trends in industry can lead to delays, and in cases such as mine, to dead ends. Third, you must let go at times when staying in the game would only make matters worse. Recognizing the appropriate time to quit, when challenging times fail to subside, holds just as much strategic importance as doing your best to carry on when a possibility of success still exists. Finally, a change of direction at the right time represents not a failure, but a necessary or inevitable maneuver. Try not to view your setbacks as failures, and instead, allow these difficult experiences to empower you on your path to success.

Sometimes, the best decision, truly, is to quit. Consider a person stuck in quicksand. As she struggles more and more, she only sinks deeper and deeper. She must keep calm to find a way out and save herself. Sometimes in real life, when difficult matters appear personal, we stray from making the right decision. My situation provides a helpful example. I insisted on staying in a specific market because I did not want to confess that I had been outmaneuvered. This choice led me to achieve nothing in the end and only hurt me even more.

While quitting might sound like something one should not resort to under any circumstances, quitting at the right moment is exactly what you need to do, when you have no hope of improving your current situation. Quitting does not always equal failure. Sometimes, it can pave the way to realize your true potential.

Quitting Can Be a Good Thing

Author's Bio

Amirreza Kamalian is an expert in land

development, who offers his exclusive services of land assembly and land severance in Ontario, Canada. Amir's superpower is his ability to expedite the process of getting permits from the city. Through his unique approach and established connections, he gets the required permits with a minimum of back-and-forth and maximum efficiency. Coming from a family that has been in construction for more than fifty years and drawing on his background in structural engineering, Amir has made a name for himself as a reliable, honest, and transparent professional.

To learn more about Amir Kamalian and his company, please visit www.mdi-development.ca.

Whatever Your Mind

Can Conceive,

You Can Achieve.

Faisal Ali Khoshroo

Whatever Your Mind Can Conceive, You Can Achieve

Faisal Ali Khoshroo

In Poland, I stood in line at the immigration office, awaiting an interview to see if I could qualify for European residency. It was a Friday, the last working weekday; we would have the weekend ahead of us, and the office would be closed till the following Monday. The only catch was that my visa would expire in two days, and I would have to leave Poland unless I had my residency interview that day. Otherwise, all the money, time and effort I had invested would have been in vain. I was anxious.

The office hours were ticking away fast. There were still a few people ahead of me in the line. I engaged in a conversation with a man who was behind me. "I need a European passport," I told him. "I've been told that if you are a European resident, obtaining UAE residency becomes much easier." I wanted to get the European residency so I could eventually qualify to obtain residency in the United Arab Emirates. To be a UAE resident was a childhood dream for me.

The man said something that struck me as if it were a thunder-bolt: "I know people who have had similar conditions to you, but even with a European passport they have not been able to obtain a residence permit in the UAE."

Time was short and I finally did not make it at the immigration office that day.

The immigration office closed for the weekend, and I left Poland.

I had invested all my profit from doing business in the previous year into the application process. Now, it had all vanished in thin air. The European residency became a privilege that I refused to receive.

Childhood Love

Yes, in Poland, my intention was to get the European residency so that I would eventually qualify to become a UAE resident. However, my love story with the UAE began many years before. Actually, I attempted to get UAE residency nine times, and failed, until I eventually made it happen the tenth time.

In 2008, when I filled out my very first application form, I owned a transportation company on the Iranian island of Qeshm. My brother and I co-founded the company, and we served local businesses. It was exceptionally difficult for Iranians to obtain the UAE residency back then because of the international conflicts and hostile attitudes between the two countries. The few Iranians who actually managed to obtain residency were those with great wealth to declare, and I certainly was not one of them.

Since I realized it was impossible for me to get the UAE residency as an ordinary sales and marketing guy, I tried my chances by applying for the European passport. At the time, I believed this could be my key to immigrate to the UAE. I made my first application to Slovakia. Then, I changed my mind when I was faced with a long list of applicants awaiting their appointments. I changed focus, this time applying for Polish residency.

In total, I applied *ten* times. Every time I tried, people asked me questions like: "Have you lost your mind? Who goes after the European passport to eventually reside in the UAE?"

Well, apparently, they did not know the reasons why I could not give up the idea of living in UAE. From a young age, I considered myself culturally akin to UAE-born residents. I was raised in Qeshm Island, which is only a twenty-minute flight from the UAE. I knew I would not feel homesick in Dubai, and I had already made a number of friends and acquaintances who lived there.

Also, my love of Dubai dated back to my childhood. When I was around twelve years old, my dad took my family to Dubai on holiday. I found the city awe-inspiring. It was love at first sight; I wanted to spend the rest of my life in the UAE. To me, a boy coming from a tiny village with a population hardly exceeding 2000-3000, Dubai was a utopia. Comparing to our limited standard of living in Qeshm, families in the UAE had in-house cooks, drivers and housecleaners. Everyone owned a cell phone, a luxury that none of my family members had at the time. Also, I noticed that in the UAE , most young people owned two or three cars, while there were very few vehicles in the tiny village where I came from. These sharp contrasts between my hometown and Dubai were a great motivator for me to seek UAE residency.

More Failed Attempts

After all my failed attempts at becoming a European resident, I tried a new route: settling in Oman. I heard that thanks to diplomatic ties within the League of Arab States, those who got its residency and registered a company in Oman could get permission to live in the UAE as well. In that case, I would be able to reside in the UAE , having to leave only once in a while for a brief amount of time. That way, while doing business in the UAE, I would be able to settle my family near me in Oman.

I flew to Oman and registered my company. I needed to find a local sponsor, which I did; however, those who promised to pave the way for my residency in Oman pocketed my money and vanished. Again, I was back to square one. Oman was added to my list of failed projects. I discovered later that this development was a blessing in disguise. Successfully running a business as a foreigner in Oman was almost out of the question, as the country had extremely complicated rules and regulations for non-locals. Having been rejected, I again tried to look at the silver lining.

After so many failed attempts, I was down and despairing, but I couldn't ignore my love for the UAE. I had a deeply held belief: "If you focus on anything, you voluntarily invite it into your life." Indeed, this has been my motto for as long as I can remember. So, I kept applying for UAE residency. People around me kept telling me, "This doesn't make sense. Stop this vicious cycle of wasting your life and money."

I even took my wife to Dubai to give birth to our baby, which cost me an arm and a leg and a lot of headache, too. You see, as a child, I always wondered why my father had not moved to a modern country as many of his friends had done. I didn't want my own children to ask me the same question when they grew up. I was determined to provide my family with a more promising future by obtaining the residency of a more developed country.

A Pivotal Moment

One day, I was driving on one of the major roads in the UAE. I was waiting for the traffic light to turn green when, all of a sudden, I noticed Sheikh Hamdan, the Crown Prince of Dubai, on the side of the street. I immediately got out of my car and greeted him, which was met with his warm handshake. I was totally moved by this experience because I thought to myself, "You just approached this country's prince and exchanged words with him. It's not too difficult to obtain residency in this country." This made me even more determined to work toward my goal more doggedly than before.

My perseverance might have seemed strange to a lot of people around me. However, that didn't bother me too much. I have always stood out among my family and friends because of my unique way of thinking. When I was a child, unlike my siblings who were into studying and education, I sold chocolate bars to the guests that visited our village. I also sold candies, chewing gum, and other stuff to children in the neighborhood. I left high school after a car accident in my junior year. I have also made strange business decisions that sounded crazy to my peers at the time. For example, when I wanted to establish a company with my brother to distribute food and healthcare products, I sold all my cars and my boat and invested all the money I had in that new venture.

"You are crazy; you will fail," a friend warned me.

I proved him wrong, of course.

My point is this: I kept applying for UAE residency despite all the advice I was given. Some time along the way, I read the DUBAI ruler's book entitled *My Vision*. I was curious to know how he managed to build a modern country on the shifting sands of a desert. I really wanted to figure out how desert dwellers had become space travelers in a few short decades. The DUBAI ruler and prime minister of the UAE, Mohamed Ben Rashid, made it clear: Changing one's attitude and hard work are the keys to achieving anything in life.

I arrived at this conclusion: "If I change my attitude, augment my knowledge, improve my skills and develop my social connections with more influential, more affluent and more knowledgeable people, I will be able to accomplish what I have been planning."

In that same book, Mohamad Ben Rashid writes, "Missing a shot to wait for the next opportunity is nothing short of sheer stupidity."

Even after my company started to make a profit and I was making a small fortune, my applications for UAE residency did not get anywhere. They kept asking me for more and more convincing financial statements. Yet, whatever I provided apparently didn't meet the required standards. Nonetheless, I kept pushing hard.

I found a legal team to help with my case and present it as best they could. Finally, after prolonged follow-ups, we succeeded. I finally had my UAE residence issued and registered my business. When my dream eventually came true, deep inside, I thanked the heavens. It was exactly then that I reminded myself, "Whatever you can conceive in your mind and believe, you can achieve." Later, I realized the Napoleon Hill had mentioned the same concept in his classic book *Think and Grow Rich*, published decades before.

Lessons Learned

I believe if you tend to dream about something, then there must be a rationale behind it. You might fail in your first attempts to achieve that goal, but you can creatively work it out if you give it your all and just don't give up. The following are the factors that helped me get past nine failed attempts and persevere until I finally accomplished my goal:

Firstly, I have been always optimistic. I was never afraid of being different or being judged. I remember when I was in grade school, my teacher punished me for a lame reason, and told me, after class, that he couldn't imagine a bright future for me. "You will end up an addict who will achieve nothing significant in his life," he said. That was exactly when I decided to prove him wrong and show him who I really was.

Years have gone by, and now I have a thriving company with more than thirty people on staff. Don't get me wrong. There have been lots of moments when I felt hopeless. However, at those same moments, I envisioned my desired future and tried to picture myself having reached my goals. This helped me change my emotional state and get back "in the groove" pretty quickly. DUBAI's leader says, "You have two choices: Either enjoy your dreams while sleeping or strive to make your dreams a reality when you are awake."

The second factor playing a substantial role in my success was that I invested a lot in personal and professional development. Even though I have found it to be expensive at times, I believe it is worth every penny when you spend money on training and education so you can become a respected leader in your field.

Lastly, I believe every ambitious individual needs to have a coach or mentor. I have had the privilege of a caring mentor throughout these years (he has specifically asked me to keep his name secret). My mentor helped me improve considerably in terms of personality, business and social relationships. Whenever I shared my concerns with him, he provided me with the best guidance rooted in his high levels of knowledge, education and experience. And this has definitely helped me make better decisions along the way.

In general, I have always tried to surround myself with ambitious, successful people. This has proved to be very effective, especially when I lost motivation along the way or needed some boost of energy when things weren't going exactly right.

In summary, I believe we must remove the prefix *im-* from the word impossible. If we believe humans are the superior species, we must never settle for the ordinary. Most people say, "Have a goal so big that it wakes you up in the morning," but I say, "Have a goal so big that excites you to such an extent it won't allow you to sleep at night." Going after our big dreams is the only way to fulfill our destiny. And this is always possible if you never give up.

Whatever Your Mind Can Conceive, You Can Achieve

Author's Bio

Faisal Ali Khoshroo is an entrepreneur, businessman, business coach and owner of a food distribution company who has managed to register the largest food distribution company in his region with strenuously continuous effort and perseverance. Through his skillset of negotiation powers, perseverance, and careful planning, he has been running several reputable brands from around the world through franchising, and his goal is to deliver world-class products to customers and consumers. Having established a company in the United Arab Emirates in the field of food distribution, his next goal is entrepreneurship and food manufacturing in this country.

Faisal is also active in the field of business coaching. He

supports and helps small enterprises and businesses, passionately providing his clients with his professional experience. His vision of a better world goes so far as to providing top-notch coaching services to small businesses free of charge. He is an energetic and tireless young man who likes to turn the impossible into the possible, always on the qui vive for new information and training in business. He passionately believes that the impossible is only for those who lack willpower.

"We love the impossible and the challenges. The impossibility of things is the justification of the weak", he always quotes from the Prime Minister of the UAE, Sheikh Mohammed Bin Rashid, and he has made it his motto.

Building Resilient Team Dynamics:

Preventing Culture from Eating Strategy

Marie-Josée Lévesque

Building Resilient Team Dynamics: Preventing Culture from Eating Strategy

Marie-Josée Lévesque

If the terms team and dynamics spoken together make you shudder, read on. There is abundant literature on the topic of team dynamics, and yet, Peter Drucker's famous saying about culture eating strategy for breakfast any day remains commonplace. When business leaders want to talk about team dynamics it is often because they have gone awry.

A business is a human system or culture, like a society on a smaller scale. The quality of the interactions between people is the mechanism by which a culture is created. Like most systems, left unchecked, a business culture tends toward chaos.

How does one intentionally create productive team dynamics that serve customers, business leaders and their teams? In other words, how do you go about creating a resilient culture?

What is Eating Your Strategy?

It is useful to start with understanding what is eating strategy; namely, gossip, social cliques, internal competition, silos, high levels of stress, low levels of trust, and tolerance of unproductive behaviours.

Gossip and Social Cliques

Gossip is a sense-making exercise that occurs when informational gaps exist. Irregular formal communications create higher reliance on more passive ways to relay information to team members, which often results in a perceived lack of transparency from the leadership team. It also leaves informational gaps that employees feel an urge to fill. This is how workplace-related gossip often starts.

One problem with gossip is that the information traded during a gossiping session is speculative and rooted in a partial or skewed view of reality. Gossip erodes trust, creates resistance to work in teams, and leads to withholding of information. Management is often required to step in to appease, course-correct, and adjudicate. Energy is wasted and synergies are lost.

Gossips are generally unaware of the negative impacts of their behaviour or simply lack the self-leadership to stop themselves from gossiping. Individuals listening to gossips enable the behaviour. They too can be unaware of their role or just don't know how to tell their gossiping colleague to stop.

Internal Competition and Established Silos

When communications between management and the rest of the team is leaving informational gaps open and gossip is common, team members start working in silos and suffering from a specialized view. These two factors combined can hinder an individual's ability to perceive fully the organization's strategy, as well as understanding the part they play in it. They will start to act in more self-serving ways.

There is a common limiting belief that a cohesiveness at management level trickles down to the rest of the organization.

It will not, unless management creates a rallying message and common objectives to achieve together and creates a positive and forward-looking conversation related to employee empowerment, higher performance, and job satisfaction (Avey, Hughes, Norman, and Luthans, 2008).

If teams work in silos while management appears united, an unintended and pervasive effect is the creation of a fault line between levels in a business. Reducing the gap and unifying the entire team requires re-establishing trust between colleagues, increasing open communication, and promoting multi-directional flow of information.

High Stress and Low Levels of Trust

Internal competition and silos create insecurity about the future, and team members can start to fear for their jobs. During times of uncertainty, stressed employees feel unsafe to express ideas, ask questions, or bring concerns forward. Cynicism wins the day, and staffs feel disengaged and left out of the decision-making process. Seeking ways to develop more participatory practices in processes where employees do possess expert knowledge will make the team and the organization more resilient.

An easy way to relieve stress is to acknowledge or celebrate successes, whether collective or individual. Acknowledging one's contribution to the overall success of the organisation, regardless of where they are situated in the organisational chart, sends a strong message that everyone's work matters.

High stress levels combined with lower levels of self-awareness and self-leadership can spell disaster for relationships anywhere, including the workplace. These are perfect conditions for the brain to revert to what it does best: identifying threats and initiating a fight-or-flight response. This means that some individuals can feel manipulated or oppressed while others would undoubtedly be perceived as pushy or bullying. Trust is easy to lose and becomes difficult to regain.

When trust is a scarce resource, staff members prefer to keep company with those they know best. As a result, a barrier is created between individual competence and organizational potential.

Tolerance of Unproductive Behaviour

Employee performance is linked to empowerment and self-determination (Drake, Wong, and Salter, 2007), and that empowerment influences trust levels between employees and supervisors (Moye and Henkin, 2006). Increasing employee confidence can be as simple as saying "well done" or highlighting strong skills. The impact is higher if the feedback is provided on a regular basis and formulated constructively.

The yearning for self-actualization is universal and sits at the top of Maslow's hierarchy of needs. Ultimately, empowered employees feel responsible and accountable for their own actions and work. The role of people-managers is to adopt behaviours and practices that empower team members.

Limiting the definition of employee performance to work output results in unchallenged, undesirable behaviours. This may be the most important enabling factor for gossiping and power plays in the office.

Culprits of undesirable behaviours are undoubtedly well-known (and probably a minority). Allowing undesirable behaviours to continue by not addressing them with the concerned individual(s) affects other employees' sense of fairness and justice. Such interactional justice has been linked to employee engagement (Meyer, 2013). Trust in a manager can also increase or decline depending on a manager's ability to handle difficult situations successfully.

The organization stands to benefit when people-managers are equipped to carry out challenging conversations.

Remedies Combining Pill and Carrot Tactics

Change Readiness Assessment

The concept of resistance to change is starting to be challenged. People may not resist change as much as they resist real or perceived loss of status, pay, or employment, or loss of comfort (Dent and Goldberg, 1999). The good news is that cultural changes should not result in loss of status or pay. The change may be uncomfortable at first, but the gains are invaluable, both on the personal and organizational levels.

Effectively enacting change in team dynamics depends on individuals' willingness to look at their own belief systems and take responsibility for their actions, which can cause discomfort. A key element in the success of team dynamic changes resides in the leadership team's ability to make it safe for people to acknowledge and learn from past experiences.

Change Tactics

Changing a culture is possible. To do so, four types of changes need to occur:

1) transforming leadership;

2) increasing clear, open and regular communications;

3) increasing overall workforce levels of self-awareness and self-leadership; and

4) building a collaborative workforce.

Transform Leadership

Day-to-day experience in the workplace causes team members to form beliefs about themselves, their colleagues, and the organization. In turn, those beliefs inform what actions are taken, or not, which impacts the organization's results. This process has been called the results pyramid (Connors & Smith, 2012).

To transform an unsafe work environment into one where people feel psychologically safe, the leadership team must adopt behaviours that contribute to turning around unproductive beliefs. Simon Sinek speaks eloquently about the impact of working in a safe environment (TED, n.d.): It stimulates a natural reaction to trust and cooperate. Over time, individuals start acting differently and the organization's results change.

Adopting a leadership style that conveys a come with me message requires seeking others' perspectives, communicating openly and candidly without judgement, and asking for and offering feedback. Leadership explores ways to overcome obstacles and is not afraid to change their own personal views and behaviours in favor of higher organizational results. Personal courage and humility need not be in short supply.

Increase Clear, Open and Regular Communications Across Levels

A survey conducted in the United States in 2015 found the top communication issues in an organization to include not giving clear direction, not having time to meet with employees, not recognizing employee achievements, and not offering constructive criticism (Solomon, 2015).

Clarity about goals, objectives, and expectations is important to employees, as it provides meaning and direction for their work. Honesty and transparency in communications should not be construed to mean total disclosure, but a regular review of what is happening and what can be expected goes a long way to reduce uncertainty and stress levels and to keep speculative talk in check (Nefer, 2009).

The regularity of communication opportunities across the organization also needs to increase and must become multi-directional. Opportunities for bottom-up communications can be created with simple questions such as "What do you think?", "How can we improve?", or "What should we do about this?"

Increase Overall Workforce Levels of Self-Awareness and Self-Leadership

Self-awareness and self-leadership are soft skills not generally taught in schools, yet they impact one's ability to work with others. Highly competent and knowledgeable individuals may remain relatively blind to the way they interact with other team members.

One enduring myth about leadership is that it corresponds to a position on the organizational chart. Failure to recognize that each person has the power to choose their own actions paves the way for unaccountability and the blame game.

Self-awareness starts with learning about one's personal preferences. Several models exist which can be used to bring to light an individual's personality, motivations, beliefs, and emotions. Self-awareness creates a deeper understanding of the experience created when interacting with others. Awareness can lead to better self-leadership.

Learning about others' personal preferences can also become a powerful tool to enhance the quality of communications between team members, whether peers, superiors or subordinates.

Providing team members with a chance to learn about themselves and become more proficient self-leaders constitutes an incredible opportunity for personal growth that impacts an organization's bottom line.

Build a Collaborative Workforce

Positive workplaces are built on individuals' self-awareness and self-leadership as they shape social norms. Social norms always exist but are rarely defined proactively, nor are they usually communicated clearly. Keeping social norms running in the background is akin to letting the proverbial tail wag the dog.

The only way to reset social norms is to proactively define the desired team values and expected behaviours and talk about them clearly and openly.

Adjusting to new social norms requires higher levels of self-awareness, self-leadership and feedback mechanisms. Adjusting to and living by new social norms is an iterative process powered by growth mindsets.

Conclusion

Changing team culture is a work in progress. Management teams that conduct regular employee surveys maintain visibility of team dynamics, creating opportunities for conversation and adjusting course. After all, what gets measured gets done.

An employee engagement survey will probe about team confidence in leadership, relationship with their manager and co-workers, whether the work is interesting and challenging enough, how team members feel about professional growth, feeling recognized for their work and having a sense of agency (Armstrong and Wright, 2016).

References

Armstrong, T., & Wright, R. (2016). *Employee Engagement: Leveraging the Science to Inspire Great Performance* (p. 140). Conference Board of Canada. Retrieved from http://www.conferenceboard.ca.proxy.bib.uottawa.ca/e-library/abstract.aspx?-did=7924

Avey, J. B., Hughes, L. W., Norman, S. M., & Luthans, K. W. (2008). Using positivity, transformational leadership and empowerment to combat employee negativity. *Leadership & Organization Development Journal, 29*(2), 110–126. http://doi.org/http://dx.doi.org.proxy.bib.uottawa.ca/10.1108/01437730810852470

Beckhard and Harris' Change Equation: Overcoming Resistance to Change. (n.d.). Retrieved July 19, 2016, from http://www.mindtools.com/pages/article/newPPM_67.htm

Bourget, L., & Ryan, K. (1999). Twelve conditions for collaboration. *The Journal for Quality and Participation, 22*(3), 12.

Connors, R., & Smith, T. (2012). Change the Culture, Change the Game: The Breakthrough Strategy for Energizing Your Organization and Creating Accountability for Results (Reprint edition). New York: Portfolio.

Crossan, M. M. (2013). *Strategic analysis and action* (Eighth edition..). Toronto: Pearson, ©2013.

Dent, E. B., & Goldberg, S. G. (1999). Challenging "resistance to change." *The Journal of Applied Behavioral Science, 35*(1), 25–41.

DNA of Engagement: How Organizations Build and Sustain Highly Engaging Leaders. (n.d.). Retrieved July 14, 2016, from http://www.conferenceboard.ca.proxy.bib.uottawa.ca/e-library/abstract.aspx?did=7866

Drake, A. R., Wong, J., & Salter, S. B. (2007). Empowerment, Motivation, and Performance: Examining the Impact of Feedback and Incentives on Nonmanagement Employees. *Behavioral Research in Accounting, 19,* 71–89.

Hamdani, M. R., & Buckley, M. R. (2011). Diversity goals: Reframing the debate and enabling a fair evaluation. *Business Horizons,* *54*(1), 33–40. http://doi.org/10.1016/j.bushor.2010.07.007

Hersey, P. (1977). *Situational leadership.* San Diego, Calif; Burlington, Ont: University Associates.

Knight, R. (2016, July 15). What to Do When Your Employee Asks for a Raise Too Soon. Retrieved July 25, 2016, from https://hbr.org/2016/07/what-to-do-when-your-employee-asks-for-a-raise-too-soon

McMahon, A. M. (2010). Does Workplace Diversity Matter? A Survey Of Empirical Studies On Diversity And Firm Performance, 2000-09. *Journal of Diversity Management, 5*(2), 37–48.

Meyer, J. P. (2013). The science–practice gap and employee engagement: It's a matter of principle. *Canadian Psychology/Psychologie Canadienne, 54*(4), 235–245. http://doi.org/http://dx.doi.org.proxy.bib.uottawa.ca/10.1037/a0034521

Moye, M. J., & Henkin, A. B. (2006). Exploring associations between employee empowerment and interpersonal trust in managers. *The Journal of Management Development, 25*(2), 101–117.

Nefer, B. (2009). Neutralizing the power of workplace gossip. *SuperVision, 70*(4), 14–16.

Patterson, K. (2013). *Crucial conversations: tools for talking when stakes are high* (2nd ed.). New York: McGraw-Hill. Retrieved from https://login.proxy.bib.uottawa.ca/login?url=http://accessengineeringlibrary.com/browse/crucial-conversations-tools-for-talking-when-stakes-are-high-second-edition

Solomon, L. (2015). Effective Leadership. *Leadership Excellence Essentials, 32*(8), 21–21.

TED. (n.d.). *Simon Sinek: Why good leaders make you feel safe.* Retrieved from https://www.youtube.com/watch?v=lmyZMt-PVodo

Building Resilient Team Dynamics: Preventing Culture from Eating Strategy

Author's Bio

Marie-Josée Lévesque has been supporting

leaders developing their personal capacity to lead and create better work cultures through consulting and coaching since 2016. She holds an Executive MBA and is a Certified Professional Coach. She brings with her over 20 years of professional experience in Canada and internationally. MJ nurtures robust relationships, develops innovative solutions, embraces efficiency and the power of the human mind. She is passionate about the role businesses play in shaping communities.

You can connect with MJ at:

🌐 https://imtransformation.biz.

Still

I Rise...

Mitra Mohamadzadeh

Still I Rise...[3]

Mitra Mohamadzadeh

The Fall

On Thanksgiving 2018, my manager at my last workplace sat me down for a serious conversation after work. She told me, "You have disrespected our policies. This will be your last day here." Interestingly enough, she referred to the policies she had created for employees a month before, which included items such as no hugging, no use of nicknames, and no hanging out at lunch break. She told me, "Your culture from back home might find this behavior normal, but it is not acceptable here." And I was laid off the same day without any prior warning.

I was shocked to the core when my manager handed the letter to me. When I went back to my room to pick up my stuff, she put her hand on the door handle and told me to take my purse and that she would send my stuff to me afterwards. On the way home, I collapsed on the subway. I clearly remember that I was not able to breathe. My chest and lungs were blocked with a pain I had never experienced before. When I dropped to the ground, I remember people's vague faces and unclear voices around me, who were trying to help me with first aid. Shortly after, paramedics arrived.

I awoke in the hospital to see a nurse taking care of me. I then remembered what had happened. I was laid off from a job I deeply loved, had sought for years, had been trained to do, and was good at.

---

3 A line from the poem *Still I Rise* by Maya Angelou - 1928-2014

The Winter's Light

Trees are unbelievably strong. They need only light and the nutrients they receive from the earth. They fill our planet with so much life and vibrancy while asking for so little. We barely even notice them on a daily basis, taking them for granted as they are scattered almost everywhere. But I did find a new outlook on life through observing how they thrive, almost die, and thrive again.

After that moment of getting laid off, a dark period began in my life. The clock was ticking away, but I was almost at a standstill. Winter was upon us, and the ground was covered with dead, trodden leaves. I noticed how resilient the trees could be: they lose all their summer's growth when winter strikes, yet they rise again in the spring. It's never the end of the world for them. There is always the next new beginning. Resilience was the key to survive in the tree world, I discovered through long moments of pondering their nature. It was also the key to human survival, I realized through long-lasting periods of meditation and self-reflection.

I made up my mind to turn my passion into a business: training people to be resilient in the face of disruptions and crises. I had established a coaching service once before, the Academy of Change, but I was not very active in it until I was laid off work and endured a long-term depression. Now I profoundly wanted to teach my fellow immigrants to be resilient, since their lives are more prone to disruptions in a world where they are far from their origins in a new country.

Not the Beginning, Never the End

I am not a stranger to starting from square one, and if there is one thing I am never afraid of, that is to learn from my failures. For that, I am called "rebellious" by my family and "crazy" by some others. I was the first to break stereotypes in my family, with rebellious acts such as moving to another province to get a university degree and then to live abroad alone. These things are not as simple as they sound when you're living in a strict conventional Kurdish culture, where men do not communicate, there is no emotional expression allowed, and your rebellious acts might be faced with an iron fist. The masculine ruling of the men of the Kurdish tribe is, most of the time, unquestionably accepted by its women.

I remember how devastated and anxious I became when I heard of my arranged engagement to my cousin Reza. My father had already sat with his brother and arranged everything, and I was the last person to hear the news. I had to move to my in-law's town, in a far end of Iran. Reza and I had many differences, and my marriage to him was filled with moments of unhappiness, specifically when I wasn't as obedient as a wife should be in the overall context of such a traditional family culture. Over time, I made him let me work and become an Adult Literacy Teacher; then I managed to persuade him to financially support me to study for a university degree in another province. Then, I convinced him to allow me to leave the country; however, his agreement was under his primary condition of "only in an Islamic country."

That was how a new chapter opened in my life. After 20 years of being away from who I truly was, I moved (in fact I ran away with severe depression due to the still-birth of my baby daughter) to Malaysia along with my 17-year-old son to fulfill my dreams of perusing my postgraduate to get a Masters and PhD in Human Resource Development. It was there that my son found the opportunity to get his admission as an international student at BCIT, Vancouver. I could also get a parent visa, due to my son being too young to go on his own. My husband opposed me going, based on the grounds that "Canada was too far." Thus, my son went to Canada on his own.

The Wake-up Calls and the Gurus

I finally convinced my husband to financially support me to join my son in Canada. I set foot in Canada happy with the thought that I was finally in a country where women's rights were respected. I was thrilled to have to learn so many new things and started learning English from the beginner level to be able to live a fuller life. For years, my husband supported us financially, but due to a drastic drop in value of Iran's Rial (currency) he ultimately had to stop. I had already worked so hard at my educational tasks, sometimes studying up to seventeen hours a day and excelling at almost everything I set my mind to do. But now, in addition to all that, I experienced several other setbacks: I got into a car accident. I was deceived out of tens of thousands of dollars. I was on the verge of being forced to go back to Iran and never return to Canada. However, I chose to stand on my own two feet despite all injuries, pain and sorrow, providing for my son and myself. I wasn't one to be held back by such difficulties.

I experienced many dark hours, each of which I tend to see as a wake-up call. They were, for the most part, big enough challenges to force any immigrant to her knees, to believe that she is a total failure. These were some of my trials; however, I had the opportunity of being in the presence of a number of great life and business coaches who helped me transform all the wake-up calls into purposeful actions, resulting in profound changes not only in my personal and professional life but in many others' lives through me. In particular, Bruno LoGreco, who was the first coach that opened my eyes to the art of goal-setting and self-care, and Dr. Shahab Anari helped me, not only with starting the Academy of Change, but also with taking it from a small business to a sustainable, successful coaching brand with a trusting client base.

I learned many lessons throughout the setbacks I endured, the most important of which remains resilience. I am convinced that resilience is composed of a number of building blocks. The main one is the ability and the will to change. No matter when and where you are in your life, you can always choose to change and be bold in expressing yourself. The second is to find who you truly are and express it boldly and frequently to yourself. Finally, where there is a will, there is a way. You might be overwhelmed at times, feeling frustrated, particularly as an immigrant, but there is nothing that can stop you if you really have the flexible mindset to find a solution. The darkness that befalls you is, in fact, an opportunity to increase your self-awareness to unveil what you may have hidden, that part of yourself which, when tapped into, lifts you and gives you the power to overcome any obstacle. That power, unleashing your resilience, is what I now discuss in more detail.

The Power of Darkness to Unveil the Lost

At some point in our lives, most of us suffer from significant traumas and grief such as moving, separations, divorce, addiction, the sudden death of a loved one, a debilitating disease, assault, or a natural disaster like COVID-19 and many more. Resilience is the ability to 'bounce back' after encountering difficulty. Resilience does not equal strength. It is the ability to move on to a state of life better in all aspects compared to what you had before you failed. Resilience is not only key to survival and to long-term success, but also extremely necessary if you want to be happy in your life. Failure is not just an event that ends at some point. After failure comes a phase so vast that pain is too small and vague a word to encompass all its implications. The depression that comes with failure can negatively and deeply affect all aspects of your life: your health, mental well-being, job performance, parenting duties, friendship, you name it.

Many roads lead to a level of high resilience, if you need to pick one. I teach many of them in the Academy in a wide range of workshops, online courses, and programs designed for individuals and organizations with a variety of needs and time constraints. However, there are a few key tenets at the core of what I impart to others. First comes self-awareness. Increase your knowledge of yourself. Consider your mind and your body with the specific purpose of knowing how they

179

interact. Next, remember you are part of nature; thus, ponder the natural world. See how cycles of life and death interact to create the overall balance and resilience that leads to nature's prosperity. If you thoughtfully combine these two, you can restructure your cognitive behavior. What goes on in your mind and soul will align with reality, because you are in harmony with nature.

Your darkest hours are meant to make you see. This seems ironic, yet, as I have come to understand, deeply true. Failure is just a tool to help you discover parts of yourself previously undisclosed to you, let alone to the world. You never know how resilient you are and what your true capacities are until you miserably fail at something and lose everything. I initially failed as an immigrant, not knowing then that later on my abilities would allow me to be shortlisted for the Top 75 Canadian Immigrant Award two years in a row. Yes, it did happen, through resiliency. So, if darkness falls upon you, seek the smallest hint of light and use it to search for what you are meant to find in that darkness.

Still I Rise...

Author's Bio

Mitra Mohamadzadeh is an author,

motivational speaker, trainer, and a PhD candidate in Leadership and Organizational Strategy at Walden University. She works with organizations that want to create a diversity and inclusion culture that will reduce the cost of mental health and turnover and increase unconscious bias awareness. She is also a Certified Professional Coach, committed practitioner of Neuro-Linguistic Programming (NLP) & Time-Line Therapy™ (TLT), and Advanced Grief Recovery specialist for all who want to move above and beyond any kind of tangible and intangible loss.

Her coaching practice was born out of her wake-up call in a car accident in 2015 and twenty-five years of academic and hands-on experience in different Human Resources roles and Employee Training experience in Iran, Malaysia, and Canada. Mitra founded her start-up coaching practice in 2016 as mitraselfcoaching.com across Toronto, Montreal, Calgary, Vancouver, and Berlin, then grew it to a corporation called Academy of Change in 2018, an educational foundation helping organizations and individuals, specifically, newcomers/immigrants to embrace change and overcome barriers of personal and professional development.

Mitra runs inspiring keynotes, training, one-on-one coaching, group coaching, companion coaching, and online/offline workshops for organizations, teams, communities and individuals on topics of "Adjusting to Change," "Grief and Bereavement Recovery" and "Loss Awareness."

The core foundation of the Academy of Change system is:

- DARE TO GROW: personal and professional development techniques
- DARE TO CONNECT: communications skills and completing an incomplete relationship
- DARE TO INTEGRATE: filling the multiculturalism, diversity and inter-generational gap

You can reach Mitra at:

🌐 www.mitramohamadzadeh.com
🌐 www.academyofchange.ca
🌐 www.mitra.newzenler.com

Three-Ingredient Recipe for

Not Giving Up

Anoosheh Mohtadi

Three-Ingredient Recipe for Not Giving Up
Anoosheh Mohtadi

When faced with challenges, people initially tend to feel stuck. Discouraging thoughts such as, "Not again!" or "Why me?" often arise during these times, but real truth lies in the nature of growth through overcoming obstacles. Human life itself stands as proof of beautiful things arising from periods of adversity. Some people likely perform their best possible when facing pressure. Difficulty promotes hard workers to get creative and practice refining skills, or even to learn a few new ones. This experience characterizes the processes of self-development and personal growth.

I came to Canada as an immigrant in the summer of 2018. I originally planned to stay with some of my relatives for a while and to utilize their network to help me find a job. Unfortunately, this plan fell through, and I ended up with no place to stay and no job to lean on for support. Instead, I moved into a one-bedroom basement suite with a couple of my friends who only moved to Canada a few weeks prior. At this time, I felt utterly depressed and clueless. Fortunately, I did not grapple with much of a language or culture barrier, but the sudden changes in plans shook me so dramatically that I struggled to build the motivation to find another way.

Back home in Iran, I worked in a prestigious job with the UN and possessed a wide network of friends and colleagues. As a newcomer in Canada, I knew very few people and could not rely on my career for financial support. Not knowing where to start, I felt like caving into the unfortunate situation and hiding from the outside world. However, I simultaneously expected to find my calling or to receive a sign that might change my life for good! I failed to see myself as strong enough to find my own way through this situation. Originally, I had left Iran to create a better life, but now I only seemed to be letting my days pass by in despair.

My friend allowed me the space to let off steam for a few days, and once I managed to process the situation, he helped to remind me of my true identity and accomplishments in life so far. He gave me simple daily tasks, such as searching the online job market and compiling information on various options to consider for my future. At the end of each day, when he returned from work, we talked about what I had found. One day I came across WorkBC, a government organization that facilitates the process of job search by empowering people and updating them about recent changes in the job market. I ended up registering for one of the workshops coordinated by WorkBC. This proved to be a great step for me to take, as it decoded the job search process and provided tools essential for a good start.

I first found a job as a part-time veterinary assistant at an animal hospital, where I started working graveyard shifts. This schedule challenged my comfort level, but by working closely with animals, I felt as if I were taking care of my own. Both of my dogs stayed home when I moved to Canada, and I missed them dearly, sometimes even crying myself to sleep since they were not with me. In fact, many times I left the TV on all night so I could stay distracted from negative thoughts in my head. I still felt like a victim of my situation, trapped in my concerns of failing and merely struggling to survive. Unable to reflect on my purpose in life, I could only see the world as a ruthless enemy threatening my being. I lost my vision, perspective, and reasons for making this move in the first place.

A few simple factors helped me through that rough patch, and they still come in handy whenever I face new challenges along my way.

1) Perseverance: One Step at a Time!

During my first weeks working at the animal hospital, I was living day to day. I remember I often said to myself, "Only worry about one day at a time!" The hospital scheduled my shifts all over the clock, and I found it hard to manage my day around them. Furthermore, I did not own a car, so going to work using public transportation was sometimes impossible. Many times I considered giving up, but I could not bear the thought of bringing an end to my attempt at a new life. Each day felt like a real accomplishment for me. In addition, managing my schedule and creating a routine grew easier over time. I made some friends at work, learned a lot more about the job, and became accustomed to riding the night buses without fear.

This adjustment process reminded me of when I adopted my first dog, Nikita. She was only twenty days old when I got her, and I didn't have any experience of parenting a canine. I thought if I found a good trainer for her, then I could simply relax and enjoy her company. To my surprise, not only Nikita required training, but I did as well, in order to keep her on the right path. I learned two valuable concepts from that experience: Do it right and do it every day! I adopted this as the best and most concise definition of a routine.

Reader, I encourage you to continually direct your energy down the right path. I am not able to tell you how the optimal routine appears, but remember that your routine says a lot about you and who you want to be. Prepare yourself for potential failure, rejection, and disappointment. In fact, consider them part of the journey, and know there is nothing wrong with failing or not mastering anything the first few times you try. So long as you persevere, you shall improve. You might lose a battle from time to time, but you will never be defeated in the great war! Utilize your routine to be prepared and to make sure you will never give up.

2) Wisdom: Be Careful Whose Advice You Seek!

We are all accustomed to asking around when we need advice on financial or medical issues. Why is it, then, that we tend to call on our fears and old destructive patterns rather than the wisest of minds when it comes to making important life decisions? Instead of asking the "What if?" question guided by your fears, why not ask the "How?" question guided by your wisdom? I cannot imagine what might have happened during the days after I first moved without relying on those dear friends of mine. Many of us struggle with thinking negatively and letting our fears get the best of us. Tremendous value lies in having someone who you trust to give you a hand and to reassure you.

I advise you to grow accustomed to confronting your deepest fears and past unpleasant experiences. There may be no way around them. Getting to the bottom of one's fears and doubts typically takes a lot of self-reflection. Walking down the path of self-exploration, you will learn your patterns and schemas and thereby know yourself better and deeper. Once you commit yourself to the process of awakening your wise hero within, you will enjoy decision-making based on realities, rather than on emotions and past wounds. In addition, you will not only have the best advisor by your side for the rest of your journey, but you could also learn the roots of your fears and ensure they will never get in your way again.

3) Flexibility: Adapt and Adopt!

Flexibility comes in handy throughout difficult times, enabling us to bounce instead of break. I recall learning about this skill from the story of Persephone, daughter of Zeus and Demeter, who was stolen by Hermes. She was taken to the underworld and forced to marry Hades despite her will. The great loss of her mother and glorious life forced Persephone to find her identity. Her story symbolizes what we go through when we find ourselves in unexpected situations that push us out of our comfort zones. The underground world in Greek mythology serves as a symbol of depression, darkness, helplessness, or confusion, while Persephone represents an immature part of us which needs to go through a seemingly unbearable experience to overcome fears. Upon doing so, we may first be able to find our true amazing selves and then to guide other souls when they are lost.

It remains our choice whether to give up or to adapt ourselves to new circumstances. You may have noticed that people who are more pliable find their way out of the turmoil of such life events faster than others. Admitting to the pain and confusion of being lost or not having answers instantly is the first step toward calling upon the energy of our inner Persephone, allowing ourselves to grow and our creativity to blossom.

Last Words

These three basic qualities are known to us all, however, their combination truly makes a difference. Our own wisdom is the guru that guides us. Perseverance is the engine that keeps us going, making sure we do not give up, no matter what. Lastly, flexibility is what helps us adjust when we face barriers in our way.

Three-Ingredient Recipe for Not Giving Up

Author's Bio

Anoosheh Mohtadi has a bachelor's degree
in economics. She started her career in project controlling with
international oil and gas companies. She then joined the UN,
working in the capacity of financial monitoring and evaluation of
development projects in Iran as an international civil servant. She
has been working in the field of financial services and customer
experience since 2019. Her passion is to help her clients through
difficult moments as much as possible in her capacity as she
believes people can only and truly grow together.

Anoosheh supports the idea of life-long education and goes by it
in her life. One of her favorite topics is Jungian psychology. She
loves Latino dancing and cooking and believes she could have

been a chef in another life.

Contact Anoosheh at:

✉ anooshehmh@gmail.com

Skype:

Ⓢ anoosheh.mohtadi

You can also find her on LinkedIn.

From Defeat

to Victory

Alka Sharma

From Defeat to Victory

Alka Sharma

There are storms that hit you, setbacks that devastate the balance of your life, dark happenings no one wishes for. Unlike the normal everyday challenges, these are not felt and experienced at the moment of manifestation. It is only after a while when the bindweeds of anxiety and depression have taken over the walls of your mind that you realize something might have gone wrong for a while now, and you need to wake up. That's when your struggle begins, and you never know when you are going to be outside the dangerous woods, like I never did at first. Yet, your struggle will surely pay off, albeit slowly.

I write this to the women who are looking to find happiness, to connect with themselves. Women all over the world who are both entrepreneurs and housewives, whom I am sure will relate to my personal journey. I have struggled a fair amount with how I look physically, and with desperately wanting to change my life in many ways. I underwent a lot of soul-searching in order to become the woman I am today. In this chapter, I will share secrets of my journey of transformation on every level.

I embarked on a career in the fashion industry years ago, and I worked in England as a buyer for a fashion house. Eight years of my life went into working in this field. I achieved success, enjoyed traveling and loved making connections with other designers and models at every fashion show I attended. Although the job was a glamourous one, after eight years of working in the industry, I came to the realization that I needed a change. In order to have a real sense of passion and purpose for life that would truly fulfill my yearnings, there was more for me to do than work in fashion. People would often tell me, "You are stunning; you are clearly made for this job!" While the compliments felt great, a sense of meaning remained absent from my days of working in this field. At the end of the day, every single day for that matter, I felt conflicted, my mind was disturbed, and I experienced restless sleep.

My weight presented a major concern, and as I continued to put on the pounds, I started breaking out in acne, eventually experiencing depressive thoughts. Observing myself slipping into this state began to take a toll on me, and I no longer felt able to focus on my job.

A Turning Point

I suffered through this state of confusion and turmoil for a solid two-month period. During this time, my work suffered immensely, and I lost most of the great industry connections I had previously made. At this point in my life, I came to a point where I arrived at these key questions: "What is my true purpose? What do I truly love and enjoy?"

One Saturday afternoon as I walked through the hustling and bustling city streets of London, I cleared my head and asked myself, "Why am I having these conflicts? Is this perhaps a sign worth paying attention to?"

Realizing my job had taken a huge toll on me mentally and

physically, I handed in my notice at work, and from that day on, I never looked back. I thanked the universe for giving me a sign to change courses and started the next chapter of my life, moving toward finding true joy and purpose.

One night, lying in bed, it occurred to me that my life's purpose incorporated fitness. I wanted to help other women determine personal fitness goals, achieve their desired lifestyle, and overcome feelings of being stuck. First, I committed myself to making one drastic change in my own lifestyle. Gaining excessive weight truly brought about internal turmoil and led me to feel dissatisfied.

I told myself, "Enough is enough! I have the motivation and power to change my life, thereby taking ownership of my future." I thought, "When I come from a place of real inner strength, I will not only be equipped to help myself, but also those around me, including my family."

I mustered up the courage to walk into a gym. As I attempted this new venture for the first time, my mind was filled with critical voices struggling with one another. One part of me said, "Turn around and walk out. You don't fit in among these fit-bodied people." Yet another part said, "Don't you desperately want to turn your life around, have more fun, and gain confidence?"

At this point, my true transformation began to take place. As I grew accustomed to working out, it became fun, despite the times when I initially wanted to give up. Success in anything, whether fitness or business, will likely not feel like walking in a straight line. Transforming oneself, physically or otherwise, requires discipline and grit, and if achieving traditional success were so simple, we would all be rich. I listened to my fitness coach and dedicated myself to learning and making the right food choices, which proved to be a fairly simple and enjoyable process. I pondered, "Why didn't I make these few simple changes earlier?" I moved through my days, beaming with joy, picturing the ideal image of myself getting closer to my grips, and thrilled with the sensations of change felt deeply through my soul and my body. On this path of self-discovery, I realized life is too short to be stuck at a job that does not inspire joy. Leave it behind!

As I transformed physically, I uncovered another form of training within the world of Latin and ballroom dancing. This type of expression through movement spoke to me in a special way, so whether I found dance or dance found me, I further unveiled the woman I was meant to be. I began competing locally and internationally, which provided me with a deep satisfaction in having found my greatest passion, my personal purpose above all others. Showcasing my talents through dance helped me feel good about myself as a person even more. Furthermore, dance provided me with recognition, a concept I neither experienced properly as a child nor in my relationship with my ex-husband and his family.

A Vision Comes to Life

The vision to open my own fitness studio was born through my experiences of physical and emotional growth and development. I now own Alka's Total Fitness, a boutique fitness studio in Thornhill, Ontario, Canada. My mission at Alka's Total Fitness is to empower women to transform into the next greatest version of themselves.

Some key features of this studio include its intimate setting, boutique style, safe environment, genuine camaraderie, and welcoming community. I take pride in witnessing new clients, who first come into the studio feeling lethargic, and after following a customized fitness program we put together for them, gradually transform their body and enjoy the process at the same time.

Our judgment-free mentality sets us apart from other fitness studios. We pledge to make new clients feel welcome, at ease, and immediately a part of the community. No particular form of training is ever forced on a member, and each client may choose the workouts that resonate best with her preferences. I find myself often telling members, "Your fight is my fight." Since fitness is more of a journey than a destination, I aim to be committed to my clients every step of the way.

Alka's Total Fitness offers a wide range of classes, such as Aerial Yoga (anti-gravity yoga), Zumba, Pilates, Kickboxing, TRX, and more. In addition, we plan to introduce and integrate nutritional counseling and life-style coaching in the future.

In Closing

Throughout this saga, I held the firm belief to never give up on my dreams or those of the others. Upon achieving my own dream, I wanted to be a prophet of hope, so I dedicated myself to helping other women find their own passions and purposes in life. I have remained devoted to this work for the past few years.

I believe three main ingredients contribute to finding success: hope, courage, and determination. One requires hope to make one's dreams come true, courage to never give up on these dreams, and determination to live life in a desired way.

A change in mindset can bring about major changes in beliefs, about who you are or who you will become. If you are currently struggling, know there is a light at the end of the tunnel. Striving to reach that light will require perseverance and dedication; however, it will also bring about true joy through performing internal work. This chapter is dedicated to all of the beautiful women who not only yearn to find themselves, but who will walk the path of transformation in order to build a more beautiful life.

From Defeat to Victory

Author's Bio

Alka Sharma is the owner of Alka's Total Fitness.

Alka's Total Fitness in Alka's words: Alka's Total Fitness is a boutique-style fitness studio in Thornhill, Ontario, Canada. We offer a non-judgmental environment, which is welcoming and supportive of women who want to become empowered physically and mentally. We will sit down with you and build a customized program that fits your needs.

Join us if you want to:

- Increase your vital energy
- Get sexy muscle tone
- Lose unwanted weight

- Gain mental clarity

- Increase your self-confidence

- Reach goals with a lifestyle coach!

Membership options are provided at a monthly rate.

Included in the membership is one week of unlimited classes, with a bonus 30-minute coaching session. We have hands-on instructors that will supervise you and give you their personal attention.

Our products are group fitness classes, including Yoga, Zumba, Pilates, CX Core fitness, Kickboxing (teaching women self-defence), Nutrition consultation, TRX, Muscle Mobility, and many more.

🌐 www.alkastotalfitness.com
✉ alka@alkastotalfitness.com
📞 Tel: 905 747 3309

The Maverick
Mindset

Arthur Smolarkiewicz

The Maverick Mindset
Arthur Smolarkiewicz

This brief chronicle of my life demonstrates how I not only learned to "Bounce Back to Success," but also how I altered my reality and reached a higher level of self-realization. Reader, I truly believe that you can attain the same success, and the good news is that the secret lies within reach for all of us. Now, for the fine print: this process will require that you change one thing, one very important thing: your mindset. Are you ready?

I am an entrepreneur and leader of Have the Edge, a premier consulting and coaching company, whose mission is to assist organizations, CEOs, and other individuals with business performance improvement and goal attainment. At present, I feel happy and fulfilled; however, truth be told, my journey proved painful and uncertain at times. Like many others, I had to hit my lowest point prior to transforming to the life I live today.

Roll Back Setbacks with the Power of Mindset

While most people recognize that adverse events in our environment, such as natural disasters and major economic downturns, can be stressful and very costly, their impact on our psyche and behavior is not as well understood. The personal trauma from these events carries the potential to distort our beliefs and lead to destructive habits that may be difficult to shake.

In my experience, our beliefs become distorted when we allow external circumstances to dominate how we perceive the world around us (e.g. "This situation is a disaster; there is literally nothing I can do to help myself."). In addition to our thoughts, our behavior can also fall victim to challenging circumstances. Research shows that major setbacks tend to trap even the most motivated and diligent people into a cycle of unproductive behaviors, such as feeling unmotivated to do much other than binge-watch television. Such patterns will become new habits if they persist for even as little as two months.[4]

When our thoughts and actions work against us, how do we bounce back? The answer is simple and lies in how we got stuck in a rut in the first place: The Mind. In what follows, I will walk you through how the correct mindset can always bring you back to where you need to be. Bouncing back not only seems important but, in fact, it proves rather essential. However, what I really want to discuss is where you might land after you bounce back. This landing point depends heavily on choice. It will either position you within your same old reality, or inside of a brand-new reality of your own creation.

Fixed Will Not Fix You

Carol Dweck's 2006 bestselling book, Mindset: The New Psychology of Success, introduced the idea of fixed and growth mindsets. This Stanford professor taught readers that having a fixed mindset results in a belief that our intelligences, personalities, and abilities are hopelessly static and cannot be improved despite our efforts. People who cling to a fixed

---

4 Phillippa Lally, "How Are Habits Formed: Modelling Habit Formation in the Real World," *European Journal of Psychology* 40 no. 6 (2009)

mindset avoid challenges, perceive effort as unrewarding, give up easily, ignore criticism, and feel threatened by the success of others. Conversely, people with a growth mindset believe their aptitude and traits can improve with effort and determination. Those operating within this second category of mindset embrace challenges, persist with determination, welcome criticism, and take inspiration from the success of others. Any successful attempt to bounce back from a setback begins with a growth mindset; there will be no movement or "fixing" without this condition being met.

The World Has Changed; So Must I

Recall the 2008 global financial crisis. Consider the 2020 COVID-19 pandemic. The world after these events looks forever changed compared to the world that preceded them. What does this mean for us and for the optimal mindset we must employ to successfully bounce back? As stated previously, the growth mindset is an essential ingredient for bouncing back, but it would not suffice on its own to provide one with enough guidance to complete the journey ahead. Why not? Because once the world changes, the place we left behind no longer exists. Now we must change, too, and for this we must adopt the innovative mindset.

I prefer explaining the innovative mindset by using a gaming analogy. Those with the fixed mindset see themselves as forever playing the hypothetical game on the same level and with the same set of skills. Those operating from the growth mind-set believe that they will continually level-up within the game and improve their skills as they put in time and effort. However, the gamers with an innovative mindset understand that they can develop better strategies and solutions to win faster and more often, as well as to overcome their opponents more decisively. This results in the entire game being played both on a higher level and in a new way.

For most people intent on bouncing back from a major setback, the growth and innovative mindsets will provide enough support. However, in my personal experience, after successfully bouncing back on multiple occasions, something always felt missing. One day, I discovered what this was. Let me tell you my own story.

Discovering My Passion

Throughout my life I often identified as a bit peculiar, wanting to approach things slightly differently than my peers. At age 11, my family immigrated to Canada. Our new start did not lend itself to a life of abundance, and this forced me to develop a solution-oriented outlook. I rebuilt old bikes found at garage sales and sold them for a profit. I took on multiple newspaper routes and organized games or competitions among my friends to contract them to do some of my work for me. I even paid them! Thus initiated a lifelong habit of seeking out inventive solutions.

I performed well in school and earned several university scholarships. However, attending university did not appeal to me, so I left after only two years. At the time, I sought something different. I knew that I wanted to make a difference, but I did not know through what or how.

After leaving university, I decided to start my own business, a martial arts and fitness studio. Looking back on those years, I can see the role that mindset played in how I handled my business, for better and for worse. My studio resided in one of the most well-educated municipalities in Canada, and I soon realized that an opportunity lay in adapting North American freestyle karate to a more pure, traditional Japanese style to suit the cerebral and sophisticated demographic of the area. This innovation coupled with the addition of cardio classes and a weight room to my studio (commonplace now, but very rare at the time) allowed me to build the largest martial arts school in the municipality with over 500 members and 80 black belts.

Then came September 11, 2001. I am certain that I was far from the only business owner to allow the events of September 11 to get the better of me. I experienced firsthand the effects of a fixed mindset on a business endeavor. Fear, confusion, and anger ran rampant, and I panicked. Since I did not know the proper way to react to this crisis, soon my business began to suffer, and I felt like a victim of circumstance. All the while, I missed out on a huge opportunity for the martial arts industry presented by 9/11 by getting stuck in a fixed mindset. Fortunately, I bounced back. The growth and innovative styles of mindset kicked in, and I kept plugging along for another seven years. Running this karate business helped me discover much of what I found fulfilling in life, exercising my passion to help others grow and develop themselves. However, after about a decade, I realized that I wanted to return to school, complete my education, and expand my horizons into the corporate world.

The Corporate Mindset

I credit the sales skills I developed while owning a small business with "selling" my way into a Master of Business Administration (MBA) program without having completed my undergraduate degree. With this new business degree under my black leather belt, no longer a karate belt, I felt on top of the world. I quickly followed up the MBA with a Certified Management Accountant (CMA) designation. I wanted to be the next Gordon Gekko of Wall Street fame, minus the inside trading, of course. My targets included four of the world's largest professional services companies: Deloitte, Ernst & Young (EY), Pricewater-houseCoopers (PWC) and KPMG. Remarkably, the timing for my entry into the corporate world seemed perfect - right when the market crashed in 2008!

As far as big business was concerned, this period felt like a time of non-stop doom and gloom. Recruiters told me that finding a job within one of the Big Four sounded nearly impossible. I wrestled with feelings of frustration and dismay, but I committed myself to not giving up. Finding and landing that dream job became my job. In fact, it also became my next business and innovation. Drawing on my graphic arts background (pardon the pun), I came up with the idea to create resumes that resembled fancy gift boxes to grab the attention of potential employers. I did my homework on target recruiting individuals at these companies, researching their favorite activities, hobbies, and acquaintances to create more openings and meetings when my interview opportunities slowed. I implemented the innovative mindset in full effect, yet the results did not come overnight.

A full year later, I finally achieved my dream. I was hired as a business consultant with KPMG, a global organization that employs over 200,000 people and earns billions in annual revenue. My tireless tenacity paid off, which is why, to this day, this trait remains a central tenet in my coaching methodology. I will always treasure my years at KPMG. Working at this firm pushed me to new limits. One cannot help but develop and grow in such an environment, surrounded by top-notch professionals on all sides. This first experience in the corporate world allowed me to explore my passion for helping people and organizations, but on a whole new level. I hold zero feelings of regret about my time there, though yet again, I eventually felt the need to move on. The classic break-up line comes to mind: "It's not you; it's me." In truth, I ultimately felt that the big consulting world did not allow me the level of intimacy with my clients and customers that I found so personally rewarding in my karate business.

My Pivot Point

My exit from KPMG, as with my departures from university and my own small business, stemmed from a desire to do something different. I subsequently took on a senior executive role in a rapidly growing service organization. Its previous record of year-over-year growth abruptly halted during an international expansion gone wrong that resulted in numerous layoffs. I found myself among the unfortunate ones who received dismissals. One month later, the other shoe dropped, and my marriage fell apart. This combination of personal and professional setbacks seriously impacted my confidence, drive, and financial situation. During this challenging time, I began questioning if I had made the right choices along the way. Though the answer did not appear immediately, it did come back as a "yes." Deep down, I still maintained a beautiful vision for myself, and it was time to bring it to fruition.

Mindset Is the Key

At this point in my story, I truly felt like my life had broken into pieces, so I began the somewhat painful process of piecing it back together. I hired coaches, took personal development courses, and even sought the counsel of a monk who previously worked with the Dalai Lama. My professional confidence returned after I helped several companies with expansion and restructuring.

Around this time, I began to study and further explore the area of mindset. I discovered the innumerable ways in which applying the correct mindset could literally transform a business or an individual's performance. Though the concept might sound overly simple, an incorrect mindset is so often the root cause of one's failure. Over time, this simple discovery grew into a full methodology termed "Have the Edge" and is used by my company to pair technical solutions with the proper mindsets needed for optimal performance. While I have great respect for my peers in the business consulting world, I believe the industry often conducts itself in a rigid and formulaic manner. Therefore, the corporate sector suffers from an unfortunate blind spot regarding the role of mindset in day-to-day operations and overall performance. Reader, ultimately, I aim to teach you and the business consulting world about the Maverick Mindset.

A Whole New Game

What is the Maverick Mindset? Let us return to the gaming analogy. Sometimes life leaves us dissatisfied with the game itself, and it takes a maverick to create a different and better game. I feel so strongly that the mindset factor represents the edge that traditional business consulting misses out on. I suppose I consider myself a bit of a maverick for deciding I might change the game and enable others to "Have the Edge!"

The Maverick Mindset

The Maverick Mindset supports us in pursuit of our vision of creating an updated game without compromise or apology. Mavericks exist in all professions and industries. Disruptors in a sense, they introduce to the world solutions that defy business-as-usual. Mavericks laid the foundation for commonplace modern experiences such as driving cars, flying airplanes, going into space, and using computers. I stand convinced that the Maverick Mindset rests within reach of us all. Reader, if you believe you have been called down the path of the maverick, allow me to share my tips for preparing yourself to adopt this potent mindset:

Monitor your natural tendency to limit the scope and scale of your vision.

Be vigilant about remaining open to unconventional ideas.

Embrace each failed attempt as pushing you one step closer to your goal.

Train your mind's eye to see past the possible to what may be considered impossible.

Challenge the rules and refuse to play by the ones that fail your challenge.

Find a way to become energized by the criticism of others.

If you can find them, surround yourself with other mavericks.

If you do not have a supportive network, get one (you will need it).

Love the journey as much as the destination!

Embracing the Maverick Mindset will not suit everyone; however, it worked for me and maybe it will for you, too. Utilizing this frame of mind enabled me to unlock the contentment, success, and joy I was seeking. Coincidentally, prior to my discovery, I received a Boston Terrier puppy and named him Maverick.

I dedicate this chapter to my mom, dad, and sister; thank you for always believing in me! To my best friend Robb, thank you for your support!

The Maverick Mindset

Author's Bio

Arthur Smolarkiewicz is the founder of the

consulting and coaching company, Have the Edge. As a man with an avid passion for helping people and organizations achieve their full potential, he assists lawyers, real estate agents, dentists, and other business professionals and entrepreneurs in reaching new levels of business performance and excellence.

His experience spans small and medium-sized organizations as well as large ones, such as I.B.M., the City of Toronto, and the Federal Government of Canada. With twenty years of experience that includes business ownership, consulting with KPMG, and holding C-level executive positions in multiple companies, he truly understands the challenges facing businesses and their leaders in today's economy. Arthur graduated from his MBA program with highest distinction and holds a CPA / CMA designation. For two decades, his greatest passion has been to inspire and motivate others, in classrooms, on stages, and more recently in online success summits with some of the industry's greats like Brian Tracy and Robert Kiyosaki. Arthur is a fervent advocate of personal development, health, and fitness and represented Canada four times on its national karate team.

Have the Edge is a synthesis of Arthur's past entrepreneurial, corporate, and personal experiences. His cutting "edge" consulting practice uniquely pairs technical solutions with the correct mindsets needed for optimal performance. While exploring the area of mindset, Arthur began to discover the innumerable ways in which, once applied, correct mindsets could literally transform a business or an individual's performance for the simple reason that incorrect mindsets were so often the root cause of their failure. This simple discovery grew into the methodology he now uses with his clients and customers. Arthur distinguishes himself with his attention to detail, personal touch, fresh thinking, and friendly, client-centric approach.

For more information about Arthur and Have the Edge visit:

www.HaveTheEdge.com.

Strong Enough

to Be Vulnerable!

Arash Zad

Strong Enough to Be Vulnerable!
Arash Zad

I was born in February 2016! Yes! 2016! On that day it was my suitcase and I, and no place to go. It was the time I moved from Dubai to start my dream life in the United States of America. I was thirty-three years old and I'd been married for thirteen years.

At the age of twenty, I started my first business, a marketing company. From then on, I'd been working diligently, trying hard to improve my life, and having consistent professional success. I lived and worked in several countries, such as Iran, UAE (Dubai), Iraq, and finally the land of opportunity, the United States of America.

Since my childhood, the USA seemed to be a country of colorful dreams. As a young immigrant, I was torn between the many and varied adventures I was dying to have and the tremendous amount of hard work needed to build my future. As I always had previously, I determined to build my future by working harder and harder every day.

Three months after moving to the USA, I started my first business. One year later, I started my second business in the financial industry, and in less than two years my team and I grew that business to occupy two offices and employ eighteen employees, with millions of dollars in revenue. We were making substantial sums of money and getting noticed in almost every nationwide radio, TV, magazine, and other media for our ethnic representation in the USA. Everything looked amazing for a young immigrant who had just moved to the country two years before. Time was flying by, and I was getting more involved in the business. I was crushing my goals, one after another. I was living the dream of every young immigrant.

Until that day….

It was February 2016, on a very normal morning like any other day, when my life turned upside down. My wife said: "I cannot continue this life; we are successful but not happy! There is no love and intimacy in our relationship, and worse, you don't even care. This is not the life I wanted to live. We have to finish it."

She was serious. I could see it in her eyes. I had known those eyes for years. I had no doubt there was no chance for our marriage anymore.

I had been so immersed in my business during the previous several months that my wife and I had literally no quality time, and I hadn't even noticed. At that time, I thought I was doing my very best, building a brilliant future for our family!

I had to either pack my stuff and leave or stay and eventually force her to leave. Obviously, I was the one to leave.

It was my suitcase and I with no place to go!

I had no clue what I was going to do. I was alone and broke. I wanted to burst into tears, but I couldn't cry. I couldn't breathe. I couldn't shriek. I was completely numb. I sat in my car without a single idea where to go. I didn't have any place to go! Not one of my friends or family had a single idea about what we were going through. I felt like a loser who had lost everything: my wife, my love, and my life. I was ashamed of telling others about it. It took me a couple of hours to find my bearings and look for a place to stay for the rest of my miserable life.

I clearly remember those days, when I began my mornings sobbing for hours and hours under the shower. By the time I was ready to go to my office, I was already exhausted.

Where did I go wrong? I was clueless about what had really happened to my wife and me. We were building our dreams, and everything collapsed like a house of cards. Those were the most painful days of my life, but they were also the beginning of the creation of a new me, born in those most difficult of days.

My wife introduced me to a family therapist, and I agreed to visit the therapist to prove there was nothing wrong with me. I wanted to somehow convince my wife to come back to me. After two sessions of me insisting on my point of view about our marriage, my psychologist asked me a very simple question: "Arash! Who are you? Describe Arash for me. How do you spend your time when you are alone with yourself?"

And I absolutely had no answer. I froze as if I had never learned to speak. That day I realized how far removed I was from myself. I didn't love myself. I couldn't spend time with the old Arash.

From a successful, loving and independent man, who was crushing his goals, I became a lonely, scared, and broke loser, who didn't even know what he wanted from his life.

It took me four years of self-discovery and personal growth to discover who I am. I went to a variety of workshops and seminars to get to know myself deeply. I dug into my past, my relationships with my parents and my wife, and I faced my real self. Every time I wanted to blame someone else as a cause of all the garbage in my life, I faced myself and my own fears. For years, I had buried so much baggage in my soul and carried it on my shoulders.

I realized how brutal I had been with myself, and I was fooling myself with the mask of success. I blindly chased success while sacrificing my love, relationships, happiness and, more importantly, myself. For this self-deceit I was paying the price. I had no other choice but to clean up the mess, and I knew it was going to be extremely difficult and painful. Nonetheless, that was the only way.

I faced all my fears: fear of being lonely, fear of being rejected, fear of failure, fear of being real, fear of loving others and not being loved, fear of not being good enough, and many others. I intentionally put myself into uncomfortable situations to deal with my fears and weaknesses. I cleared up my past with my wife and parents. I pushed myself to have some alone time, traveling solo. I set high goals and tried hard to achieve them. Each time I discovered something new about myself. I faced my authentic self at the darkest moments of my life, and I fell in love with myself. I found how lovable I am when I'm real and vulnerable.

I was blessed to have a circle of heroes who gave me unconditional love, even when I hated myself. They supported me even when I felt unguarded, tired and vulnerable. They showed me I'm lovable the way I am, not for the mask I wear. They are the people who reminded me of my strengths and embraced me with my weaknesses, no matter what.

From scratch, I created a new me, building my life again. I created a true lover, a brave risk taker, and an unstoppable go-getter. I created a new Arash who knows exactly what he wants from his life.

Two years passed, and my wife and I decided to date again. We started talking about what we desire in a partner, what are our values, what we want from life, who we are, and what love means to us. We fell in love again, I proposed again, and she said yes!

In April 2018, we moved in together and restarted our love life in our new home.

Since that day we have been intentionally creating our lives every day. We both learned the hard way that life is a journey, not a destination. Happiness comes from within, and success is not the goal. The goal is to enjoy the process. Success is a simple indicator confirming you are on the right path.

We both learned that happiness can already be found inside us. We are happier and stronger when we love ourselves and embrace our weaknesses, strengths, bravery, fears, and vulnerabilities. We learned how to stand for each other and freely unleash our true selves. As human beings, we are much more beautiful when we express our vulnerabilities along with our strengths. We managed to create a new us on a new journey.

I believe all aspects of our life are a reflection of who we are. We take the same person into business to make decisions or create relationships: with business partners, employees, clients, and others.

Do you think it is possible to separate who we are in our personal life from our business persona?

Pause for a second and take a look at yourself:

How happy are you in your personal life?

When was the last time you belly laughed?

How excited are you when you enter your office every day?

How is your relationship with your loved ones, life partner, children, and siblings?

How is your relationship with your business partner, team, coworkers, or employees?

How committed are you to your health and well-being?

How deeply satisfied are you with what you create in your personal and business life?

Do you see a shared pattern between your personal and business life?

As I was consciously transforming, I asked myself all these questions and found a common thread linking my personal and business life. I changed my attitude and behavior at work, and soon my employees started noticing. That was the beginning of a new relationship with them. They were not merely my employees anymore: they were my team, my work family, with a great sense of belonging between us all. That was the first step in creating an engaged team and motivating my company culture.

Previously, as a business owner, I controlled things in my office, and I thought that was the best way to handle the business, but I eventually realized I was killing my employees' creativity and initiative. That was exactly what I was doing in my personal life, too. I had sacrificed freedom by micromanaging everything.

Another pattern became clear. I knew success was a result of achieving goals, but I was so focused on results that I blindly sacrificed my love and relationship with my wife, and I did the same at work. Instead of engaging employees with the company goal and including their insights in its achievement, I gave them the target and expected them to hit it every time.

I learned that to avoid employee disengagement, I needed to involve them in goal setting and planning. Employees prefer to know their ideas matter and their input is taken into account. When employees contribute, collectively, a team can discern more accurate goals and plans that everyone understands and buys into. With such a team process, employees are much more likely to achieve their goals.

Company culture plays a big role in achieving high levels of productivity and is largely shaped by the traits of its owner and senior leaders. When employees are engaged, they adopt the vision, values, and purpose of the organization. They become passionate contributors, innovative problem solvers, and stunning colleagues.

As an entrepreneur, I was afraid of being vulnerable, because I thought that would limit my power of handling the business. At some point, people in leadership positions often start to avoid displaying any signs of vulnerability. After all, leaders are in charge of everything, so they're supposed to know everything. Of course, knowing everything is impossible. Leaders can't know everything about their job; employees can't know everything about their job, either. Outstanding leaders don't pretend to know everything. They instinctively ask questions. They automatically ask for help and, in the process, they show vulnerability, respect for the knowledge and skills of others, and a willingness to listen.

When leaders are authentic and real, they're honest with themselves and subsequently with others. They are empowered by and aware of their weaknesses because they have already accepted them as a part of themselves. It's a leader's responsibility to create an environment in which their team feels psychologically safe to show their vulnerability and admit they're struggling or have made a mistake, because they know someone will be there to support them. A harmonic business culture needs a true leader, and a true leader is a person who has the most courage to go to the frontline. Having the courage to be on the frontline, one needs to be empowered, and that happens when you are real and authentic. By being real and authentic, you love yourself the way you are, and that's how you can love others and create a sense of belonging in your team. Doing so will help people stand for each other in the team and increase overall productivity.

Being an entrepreneur for several years, along with the experience of working in different countries with varying nationalities and cultures, has allowed me to learn how to help businesses increase productivity and performance by creating a highly engaged team. I'm passionate whenever I see business owners, leaders, managers, and their entire teams feel they're part of a bigger vision. That's how they find themselves aligned with the company's purpose, and they do whatever it takes to see the company bloom and grow every day.

Be strong enough to be vulnerable!

Strong Enough to Be Vulnerable!

Author's Bio

As founder and CEO of ZAD Consulting Group, Arash Zad is a sought-after thought leader in the world of management consulting, leadership, and company culture. He is educated in Executive Leadership from Oxford University and currently working towards an MBA and Master of Business and Corporate Communications. His education as well as experience spans industries and continents. At the age of twenty, he created a marketing agency while studying computer science in Iran. Within the first two years, Zad was able to expand his team and open a second location. Soon after, he and his wife moved to Dubai, where Zad began working in real estate, manufacturing, and general trading, bringing in multiple six figures by his second year.

Only 25 years old, Arash Zad seemed unstoppable. He established a general trading company in northern Iraq, then became a major partner in another company where he was the youngest shareholder by decades. In 2013, Zad moved to the United States, where he launched a financial services business becoming highly successful in less than three years.

It was then that a devastating personal challenge inspired a long period of self-discovery. Realizing he had mistaken his career for his identity, Zad now had to learn who he truly was and what he valued. While the process was painful, the results were life changing. He ultimately returned to his work with a stronger sense of self.

He is now an empathetic and effective leader. Inspired to share his discoveries with other entrepreneurs, he now offers training and one-on-one guidance, helping leaders inspire greater team engagement and productivity within their team by tapping into their own strengths, weaknesses, and values. His mission is to inspire others to embrace their true selves, so that together, we can create and live in an authentic, empowered world.

Contact Arash at:

@arashzadofficial

@arashzadofficial

@arashzadofficial

Arash Zad Official

Arash@zadcc.com

www.zadcc.com